# THE GOSPEL OF JUDAS

"Beginning with the Nag Hammadi library, the Dead Sea Scrolls, and the *Gospel of Judas*, we have a trinity of essential holy scriptures that radically enrich and alter our knowledge of Judaism, Christianity, and Gnosticism. Now with his definitive version of *Judas* and its latest fragments, Marvin Meyer bequeaths the world a benevolent Judas. Meyer provides a crisp literary translation and introduction to the fully annotated *Judas* text—as well as a surprise: 'A Night with Judas Iscariot.' In his profoundly funny and thoughtful mystery play, Judas stars as the redemptive figure. Hurrah for this revolutionary book with its poetic enlightenment!"
    —Willis Barnstone, author of *The Restored New Testament*
    and *The Other Bible*


"No other recent discovery from Christian antiquity has stirred so much debate as the *Gospel of Judas*. Does it really rehabilitate Judas, or does it place him in the same role of a villain as the gospels in the New Testament? Does this gospel contain 'good news,' and if so, to whom, or does it only proclaim bad news to Judas and to all of humankind? So much has been written about this text since its publication in 2006 that one might wonder if something substantially new can be added to the discussion any longer. Marvin Meyer's important new book shows that the answer is 'yes.' Not only does he offer here an erudite account of how the new fragments change the way this perplexing gospel should be interpreted, but he also forcefully responds to alternative readings of the *Gospel of Judas*, hereby bringing his long-standing expertise on gnostic texts and theologies into fruition. Meyer's translation of *Judas* is a bliss to read: it is both accurate and accessible, in the same way as the best translations of the Bible are. The concluding, more imaginative piece on Judas effectively brings home the point that, just as the *Gospel of Judas* predicts, he really became the subject of ever increasing hatred and contempt among subsequent generations of Christians."
    —Ismo Dunderberg, University of Helsinki

"Almost seven years after the first appearance of the *Gospel of Judas*, this new presentation of the Judas text and the Judas event will delight both the lovers of fragments, who dwell on the details of language and doctrine, and the lovers of intrigue, who revel in plots uncovered and secrets unveiled. The clear prose of Marvin Meyer opens up again the world of Gnosticism to all of us with an excellent revised version and translation of this fascinating gospel."

    —Sofía Torallas Tovar, Consejo Superior de Investigaciones
       Científicas, Madrid

# The Gospel of Judas

## ON A NIGHT WITH JUDAS ISCARIOT

## Marvin Meyer

CASCADE *Books* • Eugene, Oregon

THE GOSPEL OF JUDAS
On a Night with Judas Iscariot

Cascade Books
An Imprint of Wipf and Stock Publishers
199 W. 8th Ave., Suite 3
Eugene, OR 97401
www.wipfandstock.com

ISBN 13: 978-1-61097-371-7

*Cataloging-in-Publication data:*

Meyer, Marvin W.
    The gospel of Judas : on a night with Judas Iscariot / Marvin Meyer.

    xii + 96 p.; 21.5 cm.—Includes bibliographic references.

    1. Judas Iscariot. 2. Gospel of Judas. 3. Codex Tchacos. 4. Apocryphal books (New Testament)—Criticism, interpretation, etc. 5. Gnosticism. I. Title.

BS2460 J8 M49 2011

Manufactured in the USA.

Author photo by Ed Brown.

"God caused knowledge to be given to Adam
and those with him, so that the kings of chaos
and the underworld would not lord it over them."

*The Gospel of Judas*

# CONTENTS

# ACKNOWLEDGMENTS

I would like to express my appreciation to K. C. Hanson and his colleagues at Cascade Books for their encouragement and assistance in the production of this book. I offer my particular thanks to Lance Jenott, who generously shared his research with me as he was preparing his dissertation for publication, and to my colleague Gregor Wurst, with whom I have collaborated on the publication of Codex Tchacos over the last several years and whose insightful comments have invariably proved helpful. Discussions with Hans-Gebhard Bethge, Uwe-Karsten Plisch, and Gregor Wurst at a seminar in Augsburg, Germany, during June–July 2011 have yielded a number of significant insights into the text. I also must acknowledge my wife, Bonita, and my children, who have had to endure my preoccupation with Judas Iscariot and the *Gospel of Judas* for several years. Judas has been, in a way, our houseguest since 2005, and my family has been generous in accommodating him—and me—in our conversations.

# INTRODUCTION

## Discovery

*The first night I spent communing with Judas Iscariot and the* Gospel of Judas *was in the autumn of 2005, in Washington DC, in an office I was occupying at the headquarters of the National* Geographic Society. *The office, I was told, was used by a photographer associated with the image of the young woman from Afghanistan, with piercing green eyes, who graced the cover of the* National Geographic Magazine *some years ago. Now she gazed down off the wall at me as I in turn looked at the text of the* Gospel of Judas. *Maybe she was looking over my shoulder at the text. I had been invited to join the National Geographic research team, with Coptological colleagues Rodolphe Kasser, Gregor Wurst, and François Gaudard, and our scholarly assignment was to produce an edition of Codex Tchacos, which includes the* Gospel of Judas. *When that night I cast my eyes upon the Coptic text of the* Gospel of Judas *for the first time, I was astonished to see names that were familiar from my work on Sethian gnosis: Barbelo, Autogenes (Self-Conceived), Seth, Yaldabaoth, Sakla, Nebro. And there was the startling title of the text: the* Gospel of Judas—*that is, Judas Iscariot, the disciple of Jesus damned by the Christian church as the betrayer of his master. Here, for the first time in over fifteen hun-*

*dred years, the* Gospel of Judas, *attacked by Irenaeus of Lyon and other heresy hunters as the quintessential heretical gospel, could be read and studied once again.*

The tale of the discovery, publication, and interpretation of the *Gospel of Judas* is one of the truly fascinating stories of literary remains uncovered in the sands of Egypt.[1] The early stages of the story remain shrouded in the mystery and uncertainty characteristic of many such tales of discovery. It has been suggested that the *Gospel of Judas*, preserved in Coptic in what is now called Codex Tchacos, was found near al-Minya in the 1970s, along with a codex of Coptic translations of letters of Paul, a Greek text of the book of Exodus, and a Greek mathematical treatise. Herbert Krosney, the author and journalist who pieced together the story of the discovery, describes the circumstances of the find. According to Krosney, Codex Tchacos and the other texts were found by local fellahin in a cave that was located at the Jabal Qarara and had been used for a Coptic burial. The cave contained, among other things, Roman glassware in baskets or papyrus or straw wrappings. Krosney writes, "The fellahin stumbled upon the cave hidden down in the rocks. Climbing down to it, they found the skeleton of a wealthy man in a shroud. Other human remains, probably members of the dead man's family, were with

---

1. On the discovery of the *Gospel of Judas*, see Krosney, *The Lost Gospel*. For the text and translation of the *Gospel of Judas*, see Kasser et al., *The Gospel of Judas*; Kasser, Meyer, and Wurst, eds., *The Gospel of Judas: From Codex Tchacos* (1st ed., 2006; 2nd ed., 2008). The English translation of the *Gospel of Judas* given here is based in large part on the Coptic text in the critical edition. Portions of this introduction were presented at a conference on "Achievements and Problems of Modern Egyptology" sponsored by the Russian Academy of Sciences and held in Moscow in September–October 2009. In this book most of the translations are my own. The translations of texts from the Nag Hammadi library are taken, with modifications, from Meyer, *The Nag Hammadi Scriptures: The International Edition*; citations from *Pistis Sophia* are from Schmidt, *Pistis Sophia*; the citation from Irenaeus on Judas and Sophia is adapted from the translation of *Adversus haereses* by Alexander Roberts and James Donaldson in *Ante-Nicene Fathers*.

him in the cave. His precious books were beside him, encased in a white limestone box."[2]

As the story continues, thereafter Codex Tchacos, with the *Gospel of Judas* as one of its texts, was brought to Cairo, put on display, stolen, recovered, and shown to scholars in Europe. Eventually the codex found its way to the United States, where it was stored in a safe-deposit box in Hicksville, New York, for sixteen years, then obtained for purchase by an American collector, Bruce Ferrini, who put the papyrus in a freezer in a misguided effort, it seems, to separate the papyrus pages. Such inappropriate handling of the codex clearly caused considerable damage to the papyrus. Nonetheless, the papyrus pages of Codex Tchacos have been painstakingly reassembled, and the text has undergone radiocarbon tests for samples of the papyrus and leather binding and a transmission electron microscopy (TEM) test for the ink in order to establish an ancient date for the codex. Such an ancient date, in the late third or early fourth century, has been confirmed by the scientific tests. In 2006 a Coptic transcription of the *Gospel of Judas* was made available online, and a popular book was published by the National Geographic Society. In 2007 a critical edition of the *Gospel of Judas* and Codex Tchacos was published; and following that, in 2008, a second, slightly updated translation of the *Gospel of Judas* was produced.

The conclusion of Codex Tchacos is not currently available, and it may either have fallen into the hands of some person or organization or have been damaged and destroyed. The codex as now known from the papyrus that is available must have contained at least five texts:

1. the *Letter of Peter to Philip* (1,1—9,15), a text also known in a slightly different version as the second tractate of Nag Hammadi Codex VIII;

2. Krosney, *The Lost Gospel*, 10.

3

2. a text called *James* (10,1—30,27), a version of a tractate titled the *Revelation* (or, *Apocalypse*) *of James* (and given the title *First Revelation of James* by scholars to distinguish it from the so-called *Second Revelation of James*), preserved as the third tractate in Nag Hammadi Codex V;

3. the *Gospel of Judas* (33,1—58,28);

4. a fragmentary text provisionally called a *Book of Allogenes* (59,1—66,25ff.), which is missing a significant amount of its contents, and is given its current title on the basis of ink traces and the name of the central revelatory figure in the work; and

5. a Coptic version of *Corpus Hermeticum XIII*, here known from words and phrases in fragments identified by Jean-Pierre Mahé and Gregor Wurst.[3]

There may have been more texts in the collection. As it currently is known, Codex Tchacos is a collection of revelatory texts about the nature of gnosis and the true meaning of life and death, including the life and death of Jesus.

## Judas and Irenaeus

*Rodolphe Kasser, the distinguished Swiss Coptologist and papyrologist who was the senior member of the National Geographic research team, recalls that when he first saw the text of Codex Tchacos in 2001, he let out a cry of astonishment. What once had been an intact papyrus codex with a leather cover had deteriorated into a heap of fragments piled in a cardboard box. Years earlier, in 1983, several scholars, including Stephen Emmel, currently of the University of Münster, were invited to Geneva to view a collection of codices, one of which was what is now named Codex Tchacos,*

---

3. Cf. Kasser, Meyer, and Wurst, eds., *The Gospel of Judas* (2nd ed.), 11.

*and at that time, it has been noted, the codex and its papyrus pages were in much better shape. Time and unkind hands took their toll on the codex, and by 2001 the ancient book was in shambles. The story of what happened thereafter is something of a papyrological miracle. Through the skill and devotion of Rodolphe Kasser, who was suffering from Parkinson's disease, the expertise and experience of Florence Darbre of the Bodmer Foundation, and the tenacity and computer skills of Gregor Wurst of the University of Augsburg, the boxful of fragments became a book again. The* Gospel of Judas *was emerging from the mist—and the papyrus dust—of antiquity.*

The *Gospel of Judas* was known by title, prior to the discovery of Codex Tchacos, from comments in the writings of such heresiologists as Irenaeus of Lyon, Pseudo-Tertullian, and Epiphanius of Salamis. The comments of Irenaeus, writing in his tract *Adversus haereses* ("Against Heresies") around 180 CE are most helpful. The time of his writing suggests a date of composition for the *Gospel of Judas* around the middle of the second century. (It almost certainly was composed in Greek and translated into Coptic later.) Irenaeus observes (1.31.1) that some gnostics, in a revisionist reading of the documents of the Jewish Scriptures, revere figures like Cain, Esau, Korah, and the Sodomites, precisely because "such persons are of the same people as themselves,"[4] that is, they, like the gnostics, have been oppressed by the demiurge and defamed in the holy book of the demiurge, since they are of the order of the realm above. Irenaeus moves directly to a discussion of Judas and the *Gospel of Judas*, and by clear implication he places Judas in the same camp as those who are in the know but are opposed by the demiurge and are evaluated in a negative way in biblical traditions. (This may account for the fact that in the *Gospel of Judas*, "Judas the betrayer" is the recipient of revelation from Jesus but is also opposed, oppressed, and presented as the

---

4. Here and below the translation of Irenaeus is by Gregor Wurst, in Kasser, Meyer, and Wurst, eds., *The Gospel of Judas* (2nd ed.), 170.

one who sacrifices the mortal body Jesus has been using.) "Judas the betrayer," Irenaeus writes, "was thoroughly acquainted with these things, they say," and in the *Gospel of Judas*—"a fabricated work," according to the heresiologist—his story is told in a gnostic version. Irenaeus considers this gospel to be the creation of those who call themselves "gnostics," thinkers that scholars now commonly term Sethians, and he summarizes the contents of the *Gospel of Judas* by focusing upon the knowledge possessed by Judas Iscariot: "he alone was acquainted with the truth as no others were, and so accomplished the mystery of the betrayal. By him all things, both earthly and heavenly, were thrown into dissolution."

While it is unlikely that Irenaeus had read the actual *Gospel of Judas*, he seems to have gotten several things right about the character of the gospel. Judas is the most prominent and the most enlightened of the disciples of Jesus in the gospel; the significance of the handing over of Jesus by Judas is something of a mystery in the *Gospel of Judas*, and it merits being depicted by Irenaeus as the *mustērion prodosias* (in Greek), *proditionis mysterium* (in Latin), the "mystery of the betrayal"; the events subsequent to the betrayal in the gospel are presented in apocalyptic terms, as the eradication of evil and the destruction of heaven and earth. Irenaeus not only describes portions of the *Gospel of Judas* correctly; he even gets the sequence of events straight in the concluding portion of the *Gospel of Judas*, as is clear from the Coptic text and now even more so from newly recovered papyrus fragments of the gospel.

## Contents

*By the time the contents of the* Gospel of Judas *were coming to expression in the work going on in Washington D.C. in 2005, we began to discuss together the obvious significance of this remark-*

*able text. One day several of us gathered for lunch at a restaurant a few steps from the National Geographic buildings. Around the table were, among others, the National Geographic photographer who would do much of the photographic work in Egypt and Europe and the author who would write the article on the* Gospel of Judas *for* National Geographic Magazine. *The plans for publication and presentation were ambitious—two or three books, a major magazine article, a television documentary, a museum exhibit. I ordered a chicken salad for lunch. While we chewed our food, we engaged in an animated conversation about the* Gospel of Judas *and its implications for the history of the early church and the theological options in the first centuries of the Christian movement. How, we asked, does the* Gospel of Judas *change the story of the early church, and how does this gospel take its place among other Christian gospels, including the four gospels in the New Testament canon? Obviously the interpretive possibilities are interesting and thought-provoking, and we kept talking until the restaurant was empty. As we were about to leave, the maitre d' approached our table with a note that had been called in, apparently by someone who had been in the restaurant at an adjoining table and had been disturbed by the conversation he overheard. This person clearly felt called to defend traditional Christian faith against such an untraditional text as the* Gospel of Judas. *The maitre d' gave me the note, and I read it to the others. The note said, "God wrote a book." I turned to the maitre d' and asked him how he knew to give the note to me. The maitre d' replied that the man on the telephone had said that he should give the note to the guy with the chicken salad.*

The title *Gospel of Judas* derives from the titular subscript (*peuaggelion ᵉnioudas*, 58,27–28), and the incipit or prologue of the gospel provides an overview of its contents: "The hidden revelatory discourse (*plogo[s] ethēp ᵉntapophasis*) that Jesus spoke with Judas Iscariot during a period of eight days, up to three days before he celebrated Passover" (33,1–6). The narrative introduces

Jesus calling the twelve disciples and speaking with them about "the mysteries (*ᵉmmustēri[o]n*) that transcend the world and what is going to happen at the end" (33,16–18).

One day, it is said, Jesus happens upon the disciples as they are celebrating a sacred meal reminiscent of the Passover meal or the eucharist, and he laughs. Jesus laughs a great deal in the *Gospel of Judas*, as he does in other Sethian texts as well as elsewhere in gnostic literature.[5] The disciples complain about the laughter, but Jesus insists that he is not laughing at them. He says, "You are not doing this of your own will but because this is how your god [will be] praised" (34,8–11). The disciples respond by confessing, "Master, you . . . are the son of our god" (34,11–13), but Jesus turns away from this statement of confession. They are talking about the creator of the world, the demiurge, and Jesus is not the son of the demiurge. At this the disciples are furious, and Jesus invites them to step up to him and face him, but none has the strength to do so—except Judas Iscariot. He stands before Jesus, averts his eyes, apparently in a respectful manner, and offers a profession, from a Sethian gnostic point of view, of who Jesus really is. Judas states before Jesus, "I know who you are and where you have come from. You have come from the immortal aeon of Barbelo, and I am not worthy to utter the name of the one who has sent you" (35,15–21). With a term from Hebrew, *Barbelo*, perhaps meaning something like "God in four" (that is, God in the tetragrammaton, the four-letter ineffable name of the divine), this profession declares that Jesus is from a transcendent realm far beyond this mortal world, and that the name of the one sending Jesus to this world is too holy to utter.[6]

In the *Gospel of Judas* the profession of Judas Iscariot is exactly right. Jesus, it is said, recognizes that Judas "was contemplat-

---

5. See the references in Kasser, Meyer, and Wurst, eds., *The Gospel of Judas* (2nd ed.), 30–31, and below, in the notes.

6. Cf. ibid., 32; Harvey, *Irenaeus, Libros quinque adversus haereses*, 221–22.

ing even more of the things that are lofty" (35,22–23), and so he takes him aside and begins to speak about "the mysteries of the kingdom" (*ᵉmmustērion ᵉntmᵉntero*, 35,25). In fact, Jesus speaks with the disciples as a group and with Judas privately, and much of what he has to say is highly critical of sacrifice and a sacrificial cult. The *Gospel of Judas* is opposed to the practice of sacrifice and those who oversee sacrifice, and such criticism is directed toward sacrifice in the Jewish temple and, it appears, sacrificial themes in the Christian church, specifically in the emerging orthodox church. There is no place in the *Gospel of Judas* for a traditional sacrificial view of atonement. Jesus does not die for anyone's sins in the *Gospel of Judas*, but rather he offers insight and knowledge through his wisdom and teaching. Still, what the "sacrifice" of the mortal body of Jesus does in the *Gospel of Judas* is bring about an apocalyptic conclusion to the affairs of the world.

For Judas, however, the message of Jesus is not altogether positive: he will be opposed by the others, and replaced in the circle of the twelve. He will be detained below, and Jesus laughs and calls him the "thirteenth spirit" (or daimon, *daimōn*, 44,21). (A couple of other passages under discussion in the *Gospel of Judas*, passages with faint ink traces and difficult syntactical challenges, may also add to the description of the detainment of Judas.[7]) The reference to Judas as spirit or daimon could be positive or negative. A daimon can be an evil demon in Judeo-Christian sources, to be sure, but it can also simply be an intermediate being between the human and divine realms, or it can be a spiritual alter ego, in the Platonic sense, of the sort that accompanied and guided Socrates. Elsewhere in the *Gospel of Judas* there are clear Platonic motifs, such as the observation by Jesus that each person has a star assigned to him or her, and the *Gospel of Judas* builds

---

7. Cf. Kasser, Meyer, and Wurst, eds., *The Gospel of Judas* (2nd ed.), 33, 41–42, and below, in the notes.

considerably on this theme of the importance of the stars and the place of the stars in human affairs.[8]

Judas will be the thirteenth, and he will be cursed, but eventually he will rule over the others. His star, Jesus announces, will rule over the thirteenth aeon (55,10–11). The concept of twelve aeons and thirteen aeons is used in Sethian literature, variously, but the closest and most exact parallels to the phrase "thirteenth aeon" are to be found in the *Pistis Sophia* and the *Books of Jeu*. There it is proclaimed that Sophia, the wisdom of God fallen into this world below, is persecuted by the archons of the twelve aeons, and although she is separated from the thirteenth aeon, she will return there, to her dwelling place in "the thirteenth aeon, the place of righteousness" (1.50). The thirteenth aeon retains a degree of ambiguity in the *Pistis Sophia*, to be sure, yet it remains the blissful goal of salvation and restoration for divine wisdom in the text. Further, like Judas, Sophia is referred to as a daimon, in two languages (Greek *daimōn*, Coptic *refšoor*), in the *Pistis Sophia* (1.39; 1.55). A similar situation is to be noted in Pseudo-Tertullian, in *Adversus omnes haereses* ("Against All Heresies"), where the wisdom (*sapientia*) of God is called an erring demon or spirit (*daemon*, 1.2). The fact that Irenaeus also reports that in the second century, around the time that the *Gospel of Judas* was being composed, certain gnostics (apparently Valentinians) compared Sophia and her sufferings in this world with Judas and his sufferings brings Judas even closer to the figure of divine wisdom. Irenaeus says these gnostics affirmed that Judas is "the type and image of that aeon (Sophia) who suffered" (2.20).[9] The very limited presence of Sophia or wisdom on the existing pages of *Gospel of Judas*, a text without a mythic account of the fall of

8. Cf. Plato, *Timaeus* 41d–42b, cited below.

9. See my fuller discussion of Judas, Sophia, and the thirteenth aeon in Kasser, Meyer, and Wurst, eds., *The Gospel of Judas* (2nd ed.), 146–52; also Meyer, "When the Sethians Were Young," 57–73.

Sophia from glory, could in fact be balanced by the prominence of Judas in the gospel, as one who is opposed here below but is on his way to the thirteenth aeon. Perhaps Judas, with his apparent connections to Sophia, assumes the place of Sophia in the *Gospel of Judas*.[10]

The central section of the *Gospel of Judas* is a cosmological or cosmogonic revelation in which Jesus reveals to Judas the source and destiny of the light and life of God in the universe. The revelatory cosmogony is put on the lips of Jesus, but except for a single Christian intrusion into the account—an interpolation, it seems, done earlier or later, that unites the familiar Sethian angels Harmas and Athoth into the peculiar composite figure Harmathoth, apparently to make room for the surprising reference to "[S]eth, who is called Christ" (52,5–6)[11]—the entire cosmogony is a Hellenistic Jewish revelation, an example of a mythical or Sethian Jewish vision of the universe. The cosmogony builds on materials also found in such gnostic (and, in some cases, Sethian) texts as the *Secret Book* (or, *Apocryphon*) *of John*, the *Holy Book of the Great Invisible Spirit*, *Eugnostos the Blessed*, and the *Wisdom of Jesus Christ*. The revelatory section opens with words, attributed to Jesus, that employ the Sethian name of the divine—the great invisible Spirit—and a well-attested comment on transcendence. Jesus says to Judas, "[Come], that I may teach you about the things . . . that the human . . . will see. For there is a great and infinite aeon, whose dimensions no angelic generation could see. [In] it is the great invisible [Spirit] (*p[n]oc ᵉmp[n(eum)a] nahora[t]on*), which no eye of an [angel] has seen, no thought of the mind has grasped, nor was it called by any name" (47,2–13). The great invisible Spirit, taking its place in this infinite aeon, extends it-

10. The single reference to Sophia or wisdom in the *Gospel of Judas* is at 44,4, "corruptible wisdom (or, Sophia)."

11. Here I use the translation of this passage that is preferred by the translation team of Kasser, Meyer, Wurst, and Gaudard. See the discussion, below, in the notes.

self in a series of creations and emanations. Initially a luminous cloud becomes visible, and from the cloud comes Autogenes the Self-Conceived. Next four attendants appear,[12] and Adamas, the generation of Seth, along with other aeons, luminaries, angels, heavens, and firmaments, beings of glory that emerge with myriads of angelic powers and in numbers with multiples of 5, 12, and 72, leading to 360 firmaments. There is, as it were, an evolution or devolution of light, with the light of the divine world shining downward. There does not seem to be room in the remaining lacunae or gaps in the text for a narrative account of the fall of Sophia or some other divine jolt in the progress of the light downward. The use of the numbers 5, 12, and 72 in passages on the heavenly aeons closely follows portions of the gnostic text *Eugnostos the Blessed*, which like the *Gospel of Judas*—and the *Holy Book of the Great Invisible Spirit*—lacks an explicit account of the fall of Sophia.[13]

Eventually, according to the *Gospel of Judas*, the light extends to the chaos of the world below. Through the activity of the angel El (or Eleleth), twelve angels appear to rule over chaos. As Lance Jenott suggests in his edition, "The stories told by *Judas* and the *Holy Book* present the impetus for creation as an act of divine providence intended to bring primordial chaos under the control of benevolent heavenly powers." Jenott compares this account with the creation stories of Genesis 1 and the *Timaeus* of Plato, "in which," he says, "the creator desires to bring order out of disorder."[14] Unfortunately, rebellious demiurgic beings come to rule in the world below, and their names, derived from

12. These attendants are unnamed in the *Gospel of Judas*, but four similar figures, termed luminaries and given the names Harmozel, Oroiael, Daveithai, and Eleleth, commonly appear in Sethian texts.

13. On the *Gospel of Judas*, *Eugnostos*, as well as a related text, the *Wisdom of Jesus Christ*, see Kasser, Meyer, and Wurst, eds., *The Gospel of Judas* (2nd ed.), 45, 132–33, and below, in the notes.

14. Jenott, *The Gospel of Judas*, 97.

Aramaic or Hebrew, are as grim as their megalomaniacal natures: Yaldabaoth ("child of chaos" or "child of (S)abaoth"), Sakla ("fool"), and Nebro ("rebel").[15] The rulers of this world in turn bring forth five angels, and Sakla the fool creates earthly Adam and Eve. Initially, life looks grim and gloomy for Adam, Eve, and their human descendants, but promises are given about salvific knowledge and an enduring image. Jesus says, "God caused knowledge (*gnōsis*) to be given to Adam and those with him, so that the kings of chaos and the underworld would not lord it over them" (54,8–12). Somewhat later Jesus reiterates the promise, in slightly different terms, with regard to the final resolution of all: "And then the image of the great generation of Adam will be magnified, for prior to heaven, earth, and the angels, that generation from the aeons exists" (57,9–14).

Toward the end of the *Gospel of Judas*, in a part of the text that has been plagued with lacunae, Jesus turns to Judas and says to him, "But you will exceed all of them. For you will sacrifice the man who bears me (*prōme . . . etrphorei ᵉmmoei*). Already your horn has been raised, and your anger has flared up, and your star has passed by, and your heart has [grown strong]" (56,17–24). The lines that focus upon the readiness of Judas recall poetic lines from the Psalms and even more so—Tage Petersen has shown— the opening of the song of Hannah in 1 Samuel 2, and the prediction that Judas will sacrifice the man who bears Jesus takes the sting out of the infamous deed of Judas. The one whom Judas hands over, or betrays, in the *Gospel of Judas* is not the spiritual Jesus at all. The spiritual Jesus is the immortal one within. The mortal flesh is what will be handed over, betrayed, and, it is assumed, crucified.[16] In the midst of lacunae, the text seems to

15. The suggested meaning of *Nebro* as "rebel" in the *Gospel of Judas* may reflect the correct meaning of the term, which may derive from the Greek name Nebrod and the Hebrew name Nimrod in Genesis 10 and 1 Chronicles 1.

16. Compare, with Lance Jenott and others, the discussion of the two natures of Christ (divine and human) in early Christian literature.

say—in a passage that was unclear before the recent appearance of additional papyrus fragments—that something fairly dramatic may happen in the world to the ruler of the world. Whatever may be the precise content of this passage, which we shall examine below, after that Jesus says to Judas, "Look, you have been told everything. Lift up your eyes and behold the cloud and the light within it and the stars surrounding it. And the star that leads the way, that is your star" (57,15–20). Judas looks up, sees the luminous cloud—"And he entered it" (*auō affōk ehoun eros*, 57,22–23). A revelatory voice comes from the cloud and speaks in a lacuna, and the *Gospel of Judas* comes to its conclusion with an understated account of Judas handing over Jesus—or, rather, the mortal body of Jesus. By now the spirit of Jesus is gone, having returned to the light above.

Invariably ancient texts are open to a diversity of scholarly interpretations, and so it has been, in the years since 2006, with the *Gospel of Judas*. On account of the relative obscurity of the Coptic text, the number of lacunae that have remained in the text until the present, the faint and ambiguous character of some of the ink traces, and the mystical gnostic contents of the gospel account, the *Gospel of Judas* may be open to even more interpretive debate than might be anticipated. In addition to interpretations that see the *Gospel of Judas* as a more or less typical gnosticizing gospel with a critique of the emerging orthodox church and a proclamation of salvation through gnosis communicated by the savior to and through a disciple or disciples—I offer such an interpretation here in this book—several colleagues have emphasized features in the gospel like the statement of Jesus that designates Judas as a daimon or demon, who may be understood to be in collaboration with the demiurge and who commits an act of wicked sacrifice by betraying Jesus. Thus, April DeConick has proposed that Judas is presented in the *Gospel of Judas* as an evil demon in league with the ruler of this world in a gospel that functions as a gos-

pel parody.[17] Once Louis Painchaud speculated, somewhat tentatively, that the gospel's negative portrayal of Judas, though he
is enlightened with gnosis, would suggest that the gospel means
to warn gnostics against the apostasy of returning to the ways
of sacrificial atonement and wickedness in the emerging orthodox church (the word *ap[os]tatēs*, which could be translated as
"apostate," is used in the gospel at 51,14).[18] John Turner has seen
the text as confusing and perplexing, as being out of synch with
Sethian gnosis, and he has concluded that the Coptic version of
the *Gospel of Judas* is a later text with a complex textual history,
and that it is essentially pseudo-Sethian.[19] Conversely, I interpret
the *Gospel of Judas* as a gospel of Sethian content in which Jesus
gives a series of insightful disclosures about sacrificial themes
and the meaning of life and death, through a specially selected
disciple, none other than Judas Iscariot, who is enlightened with
the revelatory knowledge Jesus imparts.

While several passages are crucial for the ongoing debate
about the overall interpretation of the *Gospel of Judas*, four may
be highlighted here. Not only are these four central to the argu-
ments raised; they also are addressed, to some considerable ex-
tent, in the papyrus fragments that have become available. The
four passages deal with 1) the meaning of *apophasis* in the incipit
of the *Gospel of Judas*; 2) the meaning of Judas as the thirteenth,
linked to the thirteenth aeon; 3) the context of the prediction of
Judas sacrificing the man who bears Jesus; and 4) the final entry
into the cloud of light and what follows.

---

17. DeConick, *The Thirteenth Apostle*.

18. Cf. Kasser, Meyer, and Wurst, eds., *The Gospel of Judas* (2nd ed.), 21.

19. Turner, "The Pseudo-Sethianism of the *Gospel of Judas*," 571–604.

# Fragments

*Herb Krosney, the author who uncovered much of the story of the discovery of the* Gospel of Judas *and* Codex Tchacos *and published the story in* The Lost Gospel: The Quest for the Gospel of Judas Iscariot, *has also pursued the issue of additional fragments of* Codex Tchacos. *He published his preliminary report of the story of the fragments in 2010 in the European periodical* Early Christianity. *There had been speculation—and hope—that additional papyrus of the* Gospel of Judas *and the other texts in* Codex Tchacos *might be found, so that some of the lacunae in the text might be filled. It was also assumed by many of us that if anyone might have such fragments, it would likely be Bruce Ferrini, who once had possession of* Codex Tchacos *and then had to surrender the codex. In 2008 Ferrini declared bankruptcy in Ohio, and he confessed that he had in fact retained papyrus pieces that he was to have returned. Krosney writes of Ferrini's actions, "He also left the court-supervised proceedings at lunchtime, with his lawyer, and returned to the court an hour or so later with something like a lawyer's briefcase and what appeared to be full page fragments inside." Photographs were taken of the papyrus fragments, and they were delivered to Gregor Wurst, who sent some of them to me, and it was confirmed that the fragments surrendered by Ferrini were from the* Gospel of Judas *and* Codex Tchacos. *In 2009, a lawyer involved in the case was scheduled to deliver these fragments to Europe for conservation, so that they might be joined to the rest of the papyrus codex; but at the airport in Cleveland he was stopped and the fragments were confiscated by federal authorities. Under the auspices of issues of repatriation of antiquities, the fragments were later delivered, not to Europe, but rather to Egypt. In 2010, Bruce Ferrini died.*

In the spring of 2009, the court case involving Bruce Ferrini came to a close, and it was publicly announced that among the antiquities he had to surrender were more papyrus fragments of the *Gospel of Judas* and the texts of Codex Tchacos. Substantial fragments of the *Letter of Peter to Philip* provide scholars with a very interesting and much more complete second version of that text. A fragment placed at the end of *James* seems to give a new and fresh understanding of the gnostic interpretation of the theme of martyrdom in that text. And a number of fragments of the *Gospel of Judas* now allow about 90–95 percent of the gospel to be legible, and new light is being shed on the four key passages cited above.[20]

1. According to ancient usage, the word *apophasis*, which is used in the incipit or prologue of the *Gospel of Judas*, can have a range of meanings, from "declaration" or "revelation" to "judgment" or "verdict." The term is used elsewhere in literature on the gnostics, most notably in Hippolytus of Rome's *Refutatio omnium haeresium* ("Refutation of All Heresies"), where the author makes reference to a work of gnosis attributed to Simon Magus titled *Apophasis megale*, most likely to be understood in a positive light as "Great Declaration" or "Great Revelation" (6.9.4—18.7). In the case of the *Gospel of Judas*, the exact meaning of *apophasis* is crucial for the text, since an incipit typically provides a précis of the work. A few scholars have imagined that *apophasis* in the *Gospel of Judas* might be taken in a negative sense, so that the incipit declares that the gospel is "the secret word of judgment," the statement of the verdict against the twelve disciples, against the emerging orthodox church, or against Judas himself.[21] Now in one of the recovered fragments of Codex Tchacos, not a fragment

20. On the recovered fragments of Codex Tchacos, particularly those of the *Gospel of Judas*, see the preliminary transcriptions and translations of the fragments published by Krosney, Meyer, and Wurst ("Preliminary Report on New Fragments of Codex Tchacos"). The translations of the fragments cited here are adapted from the preliminary transcriptions and translations that are based on the photographs of the fragments.

21. Cf. Gagné, "A Critical Note," 377–83; Schenke Robinson, "The Relationship of the *Gospel of Judas* to the New Testament," 65, 85; van der Vliet, "Judas and the Stars," 138–40.

of the *Gospel of Judas* but instead a fragment of the *Letter of Peter to Philip*, the term *apophasis* appears again, in the context of one of the revelatory appearances of Jesus to his disciples. The restored passage reads, "[Then] a revelation (*apophasis*) came through (or, from) [the] light, saying, 'It is [you] who bear witness to me'" (3,11–13). A parallel to these lines may be consulted in the Nag Hammadi Codex VIII version of the *Letter of Peter to Philip*, and the parallel text uses not *apophasis* but the Coptic word *smē*: "Then a voice (*smē*) called to them from the light, saying, 'It is you who bear witness that I have said all these things to you. But because of your unbelief I shall speak again'" (135,3–8). While the content of the revelatory words of Jesus in the more complete text of the *Letter of Peter to Philip* in the Nag Hammadi version is less than fully positive, as it mentions the unbelief of the disciples, the word *smē* is a thoroughly neutral term used several times in the sense of a revelatory voice or voice of declaration in the versions of the *Letter of Peter to Philip* in both Codex Tchacos (including the fragments) and Nag Hammadi Codex VIII, and the retention of the loanword *apophasis*, from the Greek, in Codex Tchacos 3,11 may suggest a neutral or positive understanding of *apophasis* in the incipit of the *Gospel of Judas* as well.

2. Judas is referred to as the thirteenth, whose star is bound to reign over the thirteenth aeon, and new fragmentary remains placed on the top half of page 55 may expand the scope of meaning for Judas and the number thirteen in the *Gospel of Judas*. Sethian texts, such as the *Nature of the Rulers*, the *Holy Book of the Great Invisible Spirit*, and the *Revelation of Adam*, often make mention of the history of Israel in the Sethian story of salvation. Prior to the examination of the fragments, the *Gospel of Judas* seemed to have little to say about Israel in Sethian Heilsgeschichte or salvation history. Now the reading of page 55 may be expanded with information on the history of Israel as well as the place of the twelve tribes—and the thirteenth aeon. The section reads, as

Jesus is speaking, "And they will . . . evil, and . . . the aeons, bringing their generations and offering them to Sakla. And after that [. .]rael (*p*[. .]*raēl*) will come bringing the twelve tribes of Israel from [Egypt (?)]. And [the generations] will all serve Sakla, [also] sinning in my name. And your star will rule over the thirteenth aeon" (55,1–13). (P)[. .]rael may be Israel or Istrael, forms of the name of the angel of Israel, as attested on magical gems.[22] The story of Israel coming out, it seems to be, from Egypt could well rehearse the event of the exodus from Egypt as a part of Sethian salvation history. And the juxtaposition of the twelve tribes of Israel with the thirteenth aeon of Judas may add important content to the constellation of themes surrounding Judas and the thirteenth aeon in the *Gospel of Judas*.

 3. In the *Gospel of Judas* the announcement made by Jesus that Judas will sacrifice the man who bears him has been adrift, before the recovered fragments became available, in the uncertain context of lacunae preceding and following the announcement. With recovered fragments placed, the passage on pages 56–57, though still not free of ambiguity, begins to attain greater clarity as an interpretation of the crucifixion of the mortal flesh of Jesus and the resultant eschatological events. The passage, restored, has Jesus explain, with the previous text joined with the fragments, "I'm telling [you] the truth, this baptism . . . [in] my name . . . . . . this will destroy the entire generation of the earthly man Adam. Tomorrow they will torment the one who bears me (*petᵉrpho*[*rei*] *ᵉmmoi*). I'm [telling] you the truth, no hand of a mortal human [will] sin against me. [I'm] telling you the truth, Judas, those [who] offer sacrifices to Sakla [will] all . . . , since . . . upon . . . all of them . . . everything evil. But you will exceed all of them. For you will sacrifice the man who bears me . . . ."[23]

---

22. Cf. Bonner, *Studies in Magical Amulets*, 281.

23. The four poetic lines reminiscent of lines from 1 Samuel 2 are omitted here.

[I'm telling you] the truth, your last . . . and . . . come to be . . .
the ministers of the aeon have . . . , and the kings have become
weak, and the generations of the angels have grieved, and those
who are evil . . . the ruler, since he is overthrown. And then the
image of the great generation of Adam will be magnified . . ."
(55,24—57,11). This passage incorporates another reference by
Jesus to the man who bears him. The remaining lacuna in the line
that explains what will happen to those who sacrifice to the archon Sakla almost certainly is to be restored by means of a verb in
a future tense with a third-person plural pronominal subject (or
a passive construction). One possibility, tentatively adopted here,
is as follows: "those [who] offer sacrifices to Sakla will all [die
(?)]" (56,13-14). There should be other possible readings. Such a
reconstruction could shed light on how Judas will surpass them,
in that he will live, and he will bring about events that will shat-
ter heaven and earth and cause the cosmic forces to be undone.
The concluding lines of the passage, improved with additional
text, divulge the apocalyptic events that will come on the heels
of the "sacrifice" or betrayal of the mortal remains of Jesus. The
"sacrifice" of Jesus takes on something of a triumphant character:
the ruler of the world will be overcome, and the powers of heaven
and earth will be brought down and destroyed—even as Irenaeus
states in his brief description of the *Gospel of Judas*. This seems to
be, as Irenaeus puts it, "the mystery of the betrayal."

4. As the *Gospel of Judas* comes to an end, Jesus reminds
Judas that he has been told everything, and Judas, in response
to the comment of Jesus, looks up at a luminous cloud, and
"he"—someone—enters it. Scholars have wondered who enters
the cloud, and whether the cloud is the cosmic abode of the demiurge or a glorious residence of the divine. Does Judas enter the
cloud of his master the despicable demiurge, as DeConick thinks?
Or does Jesus enter the cloud in his return to the exalted realm
of the light? Even before the recovered fragments were known,

several scholars—Sasagu Arai, Birger Pearson, Gesine Schenke Robinson, and others—posited that it must be Jesus who enters the cloud.[24] This observation reflects a reasonable understanding of the sense of the text, and it conforms to Coptic syntax (first perfect verbs joined through asyndeton continue the same subject, and the conjunction *auō* plus the first perfect introduces a new subject). The recovered fragments confirm that at the end of the *Gospel of Judas* it is Jesus who enters the luminous cloud. This portion of the text may be restored at the end of the section to resolve the issue of who ascends: "So Judas lifted up his eyes and beheld the luminous cloud. And he entered it. Those standing on the ground heard a voice coming out of the cloud, saying, '. . . great generation . . . image . . . and . . . in (?) . . .' And Judas saw Jesus no more. And at once there was a commotion among the Jews . . ." (57,21—58,8). The position of Judas as observer in the recovered text makes it clear that he has been gazing at Jesus in the cloud. Alas, the final words of the revelatory voice from the cloud of light still remain unknown, still lost in lacunae, until more papyrus fragments may be placed or found. What is clear is that Jesus enters the cloud in a manner that brings to mind the transfiguration accounts in the synoptic gospels or the ascension account in Acts 1. When Jesus enters the cloud, the stars of the disciples gather around as witnesses, just as the disciples gather around to observe in the account of the ascension of Jesus in the Acts of the Apostles, and here the star of Judas leads the way. Near the beginning of the text Judas takes the lead in his profession of Jesus, and near the end he takes the lead as witness to the ascension of Jesus.

There is, as the saying goes, no "smoking gun" among the newly recovered fragments, no fragment or reading that will determine definitively, once and for all, precisely what the *Gospel of Judas* intends to proclaim. Perhaps the hidden, mystical character

---

24. Cf. Kasser, Meyer, and Wurst, eds., *The Gospel of Judas* (2nd ed.), 52.

of the *Gospel of Judas* would preclude the possibility of a single reading, a single interpretation, a single meaning for such a text. Eduard Iricinschi, Lance Jenott, and Philippa Townsend rightly refer to "the subtlety and complexity of the narrative."[25] Yet a large amount of significant information can be discovered from the additional papyrus fragments, and the text of the *Gospel of Judas* is enriched considerably by the new material. It can only be hoped that in the future more fragments will be placed and more will be found for the *Gospel of Judas* and the other texts of Codex Tchacos, and in this way more light will be shed on these texts and traditions of the early Christian world.[26]

## The Present Book

This book presents a new translation of the *Gospel of Judas*, now with the additional fragments incorporated into the translation. The book reflects my continued efforts to produce an accurate and readable translation of the *Gospel of Judas*. It builds on my previous efforts, as well as the contributions of a number of friends and fellow scholars, with whom I have had a lively and stimulating conversation about the text and its interpretation. Such contributions now include the recent work of Eduard Iricinschi, Lance Jenott, and Philippa Townsend in Robert J. Miller's edited volume, *The Complete Gospels*; and Lance Jenott's edition, based on his Princeton dissertation, *The Gospel of Judas: Text, Translation, and Historical Interpretation of the Betrayer's Gospel*. Jenott's edition is noteworthy for its emphasis upon the *Gospel of Judas* as an early Christian gospel that may be interpreted in continuity with a variety of similar Christian perspectives on Christology (the affirmation of the two natures of Christ),

25. Iricinschi et al., "Gospel of Judas," 343.

26. The translations of the fragments remain provisional; the readings of the Coptic text need to be confirmed by direct examination of the papyrus fragments themselves.

soteriology (the crucifixion of the mortal body of Jesus as the occasion for the triumph over the cosmic powers of evil), and ritual (the practice of baptism and the eucharist). His approach merits consideration. The incorporation of the papyrus fragments in my translation allows us, at last, to have a fuller appreciation of the text of the *Gospel of Judas*, which is now nearly complete. Within the translation published here, the boldfaced numbers indicate the page numbers in Codex Tchacos, the square brackets indicate restorations of lacunae or gaps in the text, and the dots indicate remaining lacunae that cannot be restored with confidence (three dots for a lacuna of a line or less, six dots for a lacuna of more than a line). To the translation is appended a series of notes that are meant to clarify the meaning of difficult passages in the *Gospel of Judas* and offer parallels to the readings in the text. An Epilogue, titled "A Night with Judas Iscariot," presents in the format of a script for readers' theater some of the most significant issues raised by the *Gospel of Judas* and the research on the historical, literary, and theological figure of Judas Iscariot. This research on the provocative, oftentimes disturbing, and sometimes surprising traditions swirling around Judas has been invigorated by the discovery and publication of the *Gospel of Judas*, and it may provide new insights into the place and role of Judas within Christian life and thought. It may even turn out that this research may stimulate fresh discussions and thoughtful conversations in the entire Judeo-Christian-Islamic tradition about who Judas and Jesus were and how they may be understood and interpreted in the religious lives of Jews, Christians, Muslims, and other people of faith. That arguably would be the greatest of the contributions of Judas Iscariot, close disciple of Jesus and leading actor in the story of Jesus.

Marvin Meyer, PhD
Griset Professor of Religious Studies
Chapman University

# TRANSLATION

## Prologue[1]

The hidden revelatory discourse[2] that Jesus spoke with Judas Iscariot during a period of eight days,[3] up to three days before he celebrated Passover.[4]

## Jesus's Signs and Teachings

When he appeared on earth, he performed signs and great wonders for the salvation of humanity. Since some [walked] in the path of righteousness but others wandered in their transgression, the twelve disciples were called.[5]

He began to speak with them about the mysteries that transcend the world and what is going to happen at the end. Time and again he does not appear as himself to his disciples, but you find him among them as a child (?).[6]

## Jesus Laughs at the Thanksgiving

Now, one day in Judea he came to his disciples and found them sitting together and practicing their piety. When he [drew] near to his disciples [34] as they were sitting together and giving thanks[7] over the bread, [he] laughed.[8]

The disciples said to him, "Master, why are you laughing at [our] thanksgiving?[9] We have done what is right, haven't we?"

He answered and said to them, "I'm not laughing at you. You are not doing this of your own will but because this is how your god [will be] praised."

They said, "Master, you . . .[10] are the son of our god."[11]

Jesus said to them, "How do you know me? [I'm] telling you the truth,[12] no generation[13] of the people with you will know me."

When his disciples heard this, [they] began getting angry, raging and blaspheming against him in their hearts.

When Jesus saw that they did not understand, [he said] to them, "Why has this confusion led to anger? Your god who is within you and [his powers][14] [35] have become angry together with your souls. [Let] any one of you who is a [strong enough] person bring forward the perfect human and stand before my face."

They all said, "We are strong."

But their spirits did not dare to stand before [him], except for Judas Iscariot. He was able to stand in his presence, yet he could not look him in the eye, but he turned his face away.[15]

Judas [said] to him, "I know who you are and where you have come from. You have come from the immortal aeon[16] of Barbelo,[17] and I am not worthy to utter the name of the one who has sent you."[18]

## Jesus Takes Judas Aside

Jesus recognized that Judas[19] was contemplating even more of the things that are lofty, and he said to him, "Step away from the others and I shall explain to you the mysteries of the kingdom, not so that you will go there,[20] but you[21] will experience a great deal of grief. [36] For someone else will take your place, so that the twelve [disciples] will again be complete with their god."²²

Judas said to him, "When will you tell me these things? And when will the great day of light dawn for [that (?)] generation?"²³

But when he said this, Jesus left him.

## Jesus Again Appears to the Disciples

The next day, in the morning, he [appeared] to his disciples.

They said to him, "Master, where did [you] go and what did you do after you left us?"

Jesus said to them, "I went to another generation, one that is great and holy."

His disciples said to him, "Lord,²⁴ what is the great and holy generation that is exalted above us but is not present in these aeons?"

When Jesus heard this, he laughed and said to them, "Why are you wondering in your minds about the mighty and holy generation? [37]

[I'm] telling you the truth,²⁵
no one born [of] this aeon will behold that [generation],
no angelic host of the stars²⁶ will rule over that generation,
no person of mortal birth will be able to join it,
because that generation is not from . . .
that has become . . .
the generation of people among [them],
but it is from the generation of the great people,²⁷
. . . [none of] the powerful authorities . . . ,
nor any of the powers [of the] aeons,²⁸
through which you rule."

When his disciples heard this, each of them was troubled in spirit. They could not say a word.

On another day Jesus came to them, and they said to him, "Master, we had a vision of you, for we had powerful [dreams] last night."

[He said], "Why did [you] . . . and go into hiding?"²⁹ **[38]**

## The Disciples Envision a Temple

They [said, "We] saw a huge house³⁰ [with a] great altar [in it], and twelve men—they were priests, we think—and a name.³¹ And there was a crowd in attendance at that altar,³² [until] the priests [came and received] the offerings. We [also] were in attendance."

[Jesus] said, "What are [the priests]³³ like?"

They said, "[Some] abstain³⁴ for two weeks. Some sacrifice their own children, others their wives, as they praise and act humbly toward one another. Some sleep with men. Some engage in acts of murder. Some commit all sorts of sins and crimes. The men standing [before] the altar are invoking your [name], **[39]** and that [altar] is filled through all the actions of their sacrifice.³⁵

After they said this, they were silent, for they were perplexed.

## Jesus Interprets the Vision

Jesus said to them, "Why are you perplexed? I'm telling you the truth,³⁶ all the priests standing before that altar are invoking my name. I'm also telling you this, my name has been written on this house³⁷ of the generations of the stars by the human generations. In my name, in a shameful way, they have planted trees with no fruit."³⁸

Jesus said to them, "It is you who are presenting the offerings at the altar you have seen. That is the god you worship. The twelve men you have seen—they are you. And the animals you have seen brought in as offerings—they are the crowd you are leading astray **[40]** at that altar. [Your minister (?)]³⁹ will stand

and use my name in this way, and generations of the pious will remain committed to it.[40] After this another man will stand up from [those who are immoral],[41] and another [will] stand up from the child-killers, and another from those who sleep with men, and who abstain,[42] and the rest of the people of impurity, lawlessness, and error. And those who say, 'We are like angels,' they are the stars bringing everything to its fulfillment. For they have said to the human generations, 'Look, god has received your offering through the hands of a priest,'[43] that is, the minister of error. But it is the Lord, the Lord of the universe, who commands. On the last day they will be put to shame." **[41]**

Jesus said [to them], "Stop [sacrificing animals]. You [offered them up] on the altar, and they are with your stars and your angels, where they already have come to their conclusion. So let them be of no account to you, and let them [be] clear [to you]."

His disciples [said, "Lord], cleanse us from the things . . .[44] we have done through the error of the angels."

Jesus said to them,

> It is impossible [for] rivers (?) . . . .
> Nor can a fountain quench the [fire]
> of the whole inhabited world.
> Nor can a [city's] spring satisfy
> all the generations,
> except the one that is great and stable.[45]
> And a single lamp will not[46] shine
> on all the aeons,
> except the second generation.[47]
> Nor can a baker feed all of creation **[42]**
> under [heaven].

And [when his disciples heard] this, they said to him, "Lord, help us and save us."[48]

Jesus said to them, "Stop disputing with me. Each one of you has his own star,[49] and [each (?)] of the stars will . . . what is his. . . . I was not sent to the corruptible generation but to the generation that is mighty and incorruptible. For no enemy has ruled [over] that generation, nor any of the stars. I'm telling you the truth, the pillar of fire[50] will fall quickly, and that generation will not be moved[51] [by the (?)][52] stars."

## Jesus Again Takes Judas Aside

And when Jesus had [said] this, he left and [took] Judas Iscariot with him. He said to him, "The water [from (?)] the high mountain is from [43] . . . that has not come to . . . [the spring of water] for the tree . . . of this aeon . . . after a time . . . . Rather, this[53] has come to water the paradise of God[54] and the race[55] that will endure, because [this] will not defile the [way of life of] that generation, but [it will last] from eternity to eternity."

Judas said to [him, ". . .],[56] what fruit does this generation produce?"

Jesus said, "The souls of all human generations will die. When these people, however, complete the time of the kingdom and the spirit leaves them, their bodies will die, but their souls will live on and they will be taken up."[57]

Judas said, "And what will the rest of the human generations do?"

Jesus said, "People cannot [44] sow seed[58] on [rock] and harvest their produce.[59] Likewise, the souls of the [defiled] race,[60] together with corruptible wisdom[61] and the hand that created mortal people, [cannot] ascend to the aeons on high.[62] I'm telling you the [truth,[63] no authority] or angel [or] power will be able to behold those [realms] that [this great], holy generation will [behold]."

After Jesus said this, he left.

## Judas Recounts His Own Vision

Judas said, "Master, just as you have listened to all of them, now also listen to me. For I have seen a powerful vision."

When Jesus heard this, he laughed and said to him, "O thirteenth spirit,⁶⁴ why are you so excited? Speak up, then, and I shall hear you out."

Judas said to him, "In the vision I saw myself as the twelve disciples were stoning me and [45] persecuting [me harshly]. Then I came to the place where . . . after you. I saw [a house there],⁶⁵ and my eyes could not [comprehend] its dimensions. Important people were around it. That house had a single room,⁶⁶ and in the midst of the house there was [a crowd] . . . . . . .⁶⁷ Master, take me in with these people."

[Jesus] answered and said, "Your star has led you astray, Judas. Further,

No person of mortal birth is worthy
to enter the house you have seen.
That place is kept for the holy.⁶⁸
Neither sun nor moon
will rule there, nor the day,
but they⁶⁹ will stand for all time
in the aeon with the holy angels.⁷⁰

"Look, I have told you the mysteries of the kingdom, [46] and I have taught you about the error of the stars, and . . . sent . . . over the twelve aeons."⁷¹

Judas said, "Master, could it be that my seed is subject to the rulers?"⁷²

Jesus answered and said to him, "Come, that I may [speak with you] . . . . . . ,⁷³ but you⁷⁴ will experience a great deal of grief when you see the kingdom and its entire generation."

When Judas heard this, he said to him, "What advantage is there for me that you have set me apart from⁷⁵ that generation?"

Jesus answered and said, "You will become the thirteenth, and you will be cursed by the rest of the generations, but you will come to rule over them. In the last days they <will . . .> to you, and you will not ascend (?)[76] up [47] to the holy [generation]."

## Jesus Teaches Judas about the Universe

Jesus said, "[Come], that I may teach you about the things . . .[77] that the human . . . will see.[78] For there is a great and infinite aeon, whose dimensions no angelic generation could see. [In] it is the great invisible [Spirit],[79]

which no eye of an angel has seen,
no thought of the mind has grasped,
nor was it called by any name.[80]

"In that place a luminous cloud appeared.[81] And he[82] said, 'Let an angel come into being as my attendant.'[83]

"And a great angel, the Self-Conceived,[84] God of light, came from the cloud. Four other angels came into being for him, from another cloud, and they served as attendants for the angelic Self-Conceived.[85]

"And the Self-Conceived said, [48] 'Let A[damas][86] come into being,' and it happened [as he said].[87] And he [created] the first luminary to rule over him.[88] And he said, 'Let angels come into being to offer worship,' and myriads without number came to be. And he said, '[Let] an aeon of light come into being,' and it came to be. He established the second luminary [to] rule over it, with myriads of angels without number, to offer worship. This is the way he created the rest of the aeons of light, and he made them to be ruled over. And he created myriads of angels without number to serve them.

## *Adamas, Luminaries, and Aeons in the Heavens*

"Adamas[89] was in the first luminous cloud that no angel could see among all those called 'god.' And he **[49]** . . . that . . . [after] the image . . . and after the likeness of [this] angel. He made the incorruptible [generation] of Seth[90] appear to the twelve androgynous [luminaries] . . . .[91] He made seventy-two luminaries appear in the incorruptible generation, by the will of the Spirit. The seventy-two luminaries in turn made three hundred sixty luminaries appear in the incorruptible generation, by the will of the Spirit, so that their number would be five for each.

"Their Father consists of the twelve aeons of the twelve luminaries, and for each aeon there are six heavens, so that there are seventy-two heavens for the seventy-two luminaries, and for each **[50]** [of them five] firmaments, [so that there are] three hundred sixty [firmaments]. They were given authority, with a [great] angelic host [without number], for praise and worship, and [in addition] virgin spirits,[92] for praise and [worship] of all the aeons and the heavens and their firmaments.[93]

## *The Angel and the Rulers*

"Now, the multitude of those immortals is called 'cosmos,' that is, corruption,[94] by the Father and the seventy-two luminaries with the Self-Conceived and his seventy-two aeons. There[95] the first human appeared, with his incorruptible powers. This is the aeon that appeared with its generation, in which the cloud of knowledge[96] dwells with the angel called **[51]** El[97] . . . . . .[98] aeon (?) . . . .

"After this [El (?)][99] said, 'Let twelve angels come into being [to] rule over chaos and the [underworld].' And look, out of the cloud appeared an [angel], his face blazing with fire[100] and his countenance fouled with blood.[101] His name was Nebro,[102] which means 'rebel.'[103] Others name him Yaldabaoth. And another angel, Sakla,[104] also came out of the cloud. Then Nebro created six angels, with Sakla, to be attendants, and these produced twelve angels in the heavens, each of them receiving a share in the heavens.[105]

"And the twelve rulers[106] said to the twelve angels, 'Let each of you **[52]** ... and let them ... generation ... [five][107] angels.'

The first is [S]eth, who is called Christ.[108]

The [second] is Harmathoth, who is [the eye of fire (?)].[109]

The [third] is Galila.

The fourth is Yobel.

The fifth is Adonaios.[110]

"These are the five who ruled over the underworld and are the first over chaos.[111]

## The Creation of Humanity

"Then Sakla said to his angels, 'Let's create a human being after the likeness and after the image.'[112] And they formed Adam and his wife Eve, who in the cloud is called Zoe.[113] For with this name all the generations seek him, and each of them calls her with their own names. Now, Sakla did not **[53]** command ... bringing forth, except ... among the generations ... which is .... And the [angel] said to him, 'Your life and the lives of your children will last for a limited period of time.'"

## Jesus and Judas Discuss the Destiny of Humanity

Judas said to Jesus, "[What] is the length[114] of human life?"

Jesus said, "Why are you concerned that Adam, with his generation, has received his length of life with limits,[115] in the place where he has received his kingdom with limits, along with his ruler?"[116]

Judas said to Jesus, "Does the human spirit die?"

Jesus said, "This is how God commanded Michael to give the spirits of people to them while they are worshiping—as a loan. But the Great One commanded Gabriel to give the spirits to the great generation without a king[117]—the spirit and the soul.[118] For this reason, the rest of the souls [54] . . . .

". . . they (?) . . . light . . . chaos . . . seek [after] the spirit within you,[119] which you have made to dwell within this flesh among the generations of angels. But God caused knowledge[120] to be given to Adam and those with him, so that the kings of chaos and the underworld would not lord it over them."

Judas said to Jesus, "So what will those generations do?"

Jesus said, "I'm telling you[121] the truth,[122] the stars are coming to their fulfillment over all of them. When Sakla completes the time assigned for him, their first star will appear with the generations, and what has been mentioned will be fulfilled. Then they will engage in immoral acts[123] in my name and slay their children, [55] and they will . . . evil, and . . . . . .[124] the aeons, bringing their generations and offering them to Sakla. After that [Is]rael[125] will come bringing the twelve tribes of Israel from [Egypt].[126] And [the generations] will all serve Sakla, [also] sinning in my name. And[127] your star will rule over the thirteenth aeon."[128]

And after that Jesus [laughed].

[Judas] said, "Master, why [are you] laughing?"[129]

[Jesus] answered and [said], "I'm not laughing [at you] but at the error of the stars, because these six stars are wandering about with these five warriors, and all of them will perish, with their creatures."[130]

## Jesus Speaks of the Baptized and the End of the World

Judas said to Jesus, "Those who have been baptized in your name, then, what will they do?"[131]

Jesus said, "I'm telling [you] the truth,[132] this baptism [56] . . . [in] my name . . . . . . .[133] this[134] will destroy the entire generation of the earthly man Adam. Tomorrow[135] they will torment the one who bears me.[136] I'm [telling] you[137] the truth,[138] no hand of mortal human [will] sin against me.

"[I'm] telling you the truth,[139] Judas, those [who] offer sacrifices to Sakla will all [die (?)],[140] since . . . upon . . . all of them . . . everything evil.

"But you will exceed all of them.[141] For you will sacrifice the man who bears me.[142]

> Already your horn has been raised,
> and your anger has flared up,
> and your star has passed by,
> and your heart[143] has [grown strong].[144] [57]

"[I'm telling you] the truth,[145] your last . . . and . . .[146] come to be . . . the ministers of the aeon have . . . , and the kings have become weak, and the generations of the angels have grieved, and those who are evil . . . the ruler,[147] since he is overthrown. And then the image[148] of the great generation of Adam will be magnified, for prior to heaven, earth, and the angels, that generation from the aeons exists.[149]

"Look, you have been told everything. Lift up your eyes and behold the cloud and the light within it and the stars surrounding it. And the star that leads the way, that is your star."[150]

## Jesus Ascends

So Judas lifted up his eyes and beheld the luminous cloud. And he[151] entered it. Those standing on the ground heard a voice coming out of the cloud and saying, [58] ". . . great generation . . . image . . . and . . . in (?) . . . ."[152]

And Judas saw Jesus no more.

At once there was a commotion among the Jews, greater than (?) . . . .[153]

## Judas Hands Jesus Over

. . . . Their chief priests murmured because [he][154] had gone into the guest room[155] for his prayer. But some scholars were there watching closely in order to seize him during the prayer, for they were afraid of the people, since he was regarded by them all as a prophet.

And they approached Judas and said to him, "What are you doing here? You are Jesus's disciple."

He answered them as they wished.

And Judas received some money and handed him over [156] to them.

The Gospel of Judas[157]

# NOTES AND COMMENTARY

1. Codex Tchacos 3: 33,1–58,29. My translation is based primarily on the Coptic text in Rodolphe Kasser et al., *The Gospel of Judas: Critical Edition*, along with the fragments of Codex Tchacos that have been published in the periodical *Early Christianity* and additional suggestions from colleagues. Other readings are mentioned in the notes.

2. Coptic *plogo*[*s*] *ethēp*. The translation of *ethēp* as "hidden," which follows a suggestion of Louis Painchaud, parallels other tractate incipits, or prologues, for example, the *Gospel of Thomas* ("These are the hidden sayings . . . ," *naei ne* ᵉ*nšaje ethēp*). The translation, "The hidden revelatory discourse," may highlight the esoteric nature of the *Gospel of Judas* and the need to discover the hidden message of the text. The translation "revelatory" is used for the word *apophasis*, which Jacques van der Vliet, Gesine Schenke Robinson, and others prefer to translate as "judgment." See the discussion in the introduction.

3. Or, "a week." Cf. also the octave, an eight-day festival in the liturgical year.

4. Or, "before his passion."

5. On Jesus calling his disciples, cf. Matt 10:1–4; Mark 3:13–19; Luke 6:12–16.

6. Coptic ᵉ*nhrot*. Perhaps read (with Wolf-Peter Funk) "as necessary, at will" (Coptic ᵉ*nhtor*). The translation remains uncertain. On Jesus seen as a child, cf. *Secret Book of John* II, 2; *Revelation of Paul* 18; *Acts of John* 88; Hippolytus, *Refutation of All Heresies* 6.42.2; *Gospel of the Savior* 13; *Gospel of Thomas* 4. The word "child" could also be translated as "appari-

tion." Some scholars choose to emend the verb in this sentence, "you find," to read "<they> find."

7. Or, "offering a prayer of thanksgiving," perhaps even "celebrating the eucharist" (Coptic *eu<sup>e</sup>reukharisti*).

8. On the laughter of Jesus, see, besides the *Gospel of Judas*, the *Secret Book of John*; *Wisdom of Jesus Christ* III, 91–92; *Second Discourse of Great Seth* 56; *Revelation of Peter* 81; Basilides, in Irenaeus of Lyon, *Against Heresies* 1.24.4; perhaps *Round Dance of the Cross* 96. For instance, the *Secret Book of John* states, "I (John) said to the savior, 'Lord, was it not the serpent that instructed Adam to eat?' The savior laughed and said, 'The serpent instructed them to eat of the wickedness of sexual desire and destruction so that Adam might be of use to the serpent' " (II, 22). Again, the *Second Discourse of Great Seth* has Jesus state that he did not suffer or die on the cross, but rather Simon bore the cross, someone else wore a crown of thorns, and Jesus was on high laughing at the ignorance of those who thought they could kill him. Basilides likewise suggests that Simon of Cyrene suffered in the place of Jesus, while Jesus stood by and laughed. The Macquarie Coptic magical codex (P. Macquarie I 1, edited by Malcolm Choat and Iain Gardner), which illustrates a number of Sethian motifs, also mentions the laughter of Jesus, and it offers an explanation for the laughter: Jesus, it is said, who himself came down from the holy aeons above into this world, found Yaldabaoth, brought him up to the light aeons, and laughed—not with the laughter of a human being but with the laughter of God's son.

9. Or, "eucharist."

10. Hans-Gebhard Bethge and Peter Nagel suggest that this lacuna may be restored to read "O Lord" or "the Lord," thus allowing for two possible translations: "you, [O Lord], are the son of our god," or "you are [the Lord], the son of our god."

11. The disciples profess that Jesus is the son of their own god, who is the creator of this world, but they are mistaken. Here and elsewhere in the translation I use the word "god" in a lower-case form where the text seems to designate the creator and ruler of this mortal world, the demiurge.

12. Or, "Amen (*hamēn*) I say to you," here and below.

13. Coptic *genea*, here and below. This term of Greek origin may also be translated as "race," but I prefer "generation" on account of inappropriate connotations of the word "race" and current discussions on the use of the term.

14. The restoration "[his powers]" (Coptic *n[efcom]*) is tentative; in his edition Lance Jenott restores this passage to read "[his stars]" (Coptic *n[efsiou]*).

15. Cf. *Gospel of Thomas* 46: "Jesus said, 'From Adam to John the baptizer, among those born of women, there is no one greater than John the baptizer, so that his eyes should not be averted. But I have said that whoever among you becomes a child will know the kingdom and will become greater than John.'"

16. Or, "eternal realm," here and below.

17. Barbelo is the divine Mother and the first emanation of the divine in a number of Sethian texts, e.g. the *Secret Book of John* II, 4–5: "The Father is the one who beholds himself in the light surrounding him, which is the spring of living water and provides all the realms. He reflects on his image everywhere, sees it in the spring of the Spirit, and becomes enamored of his luminous water, [for his image is in] the spring of pure luminous water surrounding him. The Father's thought became a reality, and she who appeared in the presence of the Father in shining light came forth. She is the first power who preceded everything and came forth from the Father's mind as the forethought of all. Her light shines like the Father's light; she, the perfect power, is the image of the perfect and invisible virgin Spirit. She, [the first] power, the glory of Barbelo, the perfect glory among the aeons, the glory of revelation, she glorified and praised the virgin Spirit, for because of the Spirit she had come forth. She is the first thought, the image of the Spirit. She became the universal womb, for she precedes everything, the mother-father, the first human, the holy spirit, the triple male, the triple power, the androgynous one with three names, the aeon among the invisible beings, the first to come forth." The name Barbelo may derive from Hebrew (*b-arb(a)-Elo*), and it may mean "God in four"—that is, God as known through the tetragrammaton, the ineffable name of God, YHWH.

18. It is Judas Iscariot among the disciples who offers the correct profession of who Jesus is, from a Sethian point of view. On the ineffability of such a profession, cf. *Gospel of Thomas* 13 and the profession of Judas Thomas:

> Jesus said to his disciples, "Compare me to something and tell me what I am like." Simon Peter said to him, "You are like a just messenger." Matthew said to him, "You are like a wise philosopher." Thomas said to him, "Teacher, my mouth is utterly unable to say what you are like." Jesus said, "I am not your teacher. Because you have drunk, you have become intoxicated from the bubbling spring that I have tended." And he took him, and withdrew, and spoke three sayings to

him. When Thomas came back to his friends, they asked him, "What did Jesus say to you?" Thomas said to them, "If I tell you one of the sayings he spoke to me, you will pick up rocks and stone me, and fire will come from the rocks and consume you."

In this context perhaps compare the vision in *Gospel of Judas* 44–45, in which Judas Iscariot says he sees the other disciples stoning him.

19. Literally, "he."

20. The translation is tentative and the ink traces on the papyrus are faint and difficult to read. The reading of the Coptic ink traces adopted here is *oukh hina je ekebōk emau*. An earlier reading of the ink traces of the text (*oun com je ekebōk emau*) yielded another translation: "It is possible for you to attain it." Some scholars still prefer the earlier reading.

21. Or, "but that you."

22. This seems to be a reference to the appointment of Matthias to replace Judas in the circle of the disciples according to Acts 1:15–26:

> In those days Peter stood up among the brothers and sisters—a group of about one hundred twenty in all—and he said, "Brothers and sisters, it was necessary that the scripture be fulfilled which the holy Spirit proclaimed beforehand through the mouth of David concerning Judas, who became a guide for those who arrested Jesus. For he was one of our number, and he shared in this ministry. Now, from the compensation for his wrongdoing this man bought a piece of land, and there he fell face first, and his body burst open and all his intestines spilled out. This became known to everyone living in Jerusalem, so that field was called in their language Akeldama—that is, Field of Blood. For it is written in the book of Psalms, "Let his habitation become desolate, and let there be none to dwell in it." Again, "Let another assume his position as overseer." So, one of the men who have accompanied us during the entire time that the master Jesus went in and went out among us, beginning from the baptism of John until the day when he was taken up from us, must become a witness with us of his resurrection." They proposed two, Joseph called Barsabbas, who was also called Justus, and Matthias. And they prayed and said, "Lord, you who know everyone's heart, show us which one of these two you have chosen to assume the place of this ministry and position of an apostle, which Judas abandoned to go to his own place." They cast lots, and the lot fell to Matthias. And he was added to the eleven apostles.

It is also possible to restore this passage to refer to "the twelve [elements]," perhaps with the twelve signs of the zodiac in mind.

23. The tentative translation "[that (?)] generation" follows the restoration of Eduard Iricinschi, Lance Jenott, and Philippa Townsend. Throughout the *Gospel of Judas*, the phrase "that generation" (Coptic *tgenea et^emmau*) refers to the great generation of the people of Seth, i.e., the gnostics. Cf. the phrase "those people" (Coptic *nirōme et^emmau*) used to refer to the people of Seth elsewhere in Sethian literature, for example in the *Revelation of Adam*: "The people will cry out with a loud voice and say, 'Blessed are the souls of those people (*nirōme et^emmau*), because they have known God with knowledge of truth. They will live forever and ever, because they have not been corrupted by their desires, as the angels have, and they have not accomplished the deeds of the powers. Rather, they have stood before him in knowledge of God, like light that has come from fire and blood'" (83).

24. Or, "Master" (Coptic *pjois*).

25. Amen.

26. The stars are discussed at length later in the *Gospel of Judas*.

27. The phrase "the great people" (Coptic *ninoc ^enrōme*) is also used in the Sethian *Revelation of Adam* to describe certain people in the Sethian history of salvation who remain holy and undefiled: "Then the god of the aeons will hand over to them some who serve [him] . . . . They will come to that land where the great people will be, who have not been defiled and will not be defiled by any desire. For their souls came not from a defiled hand, but from a great commandment of an eternal angel" (74–75).

28. Partially restored by Gregor Wurst.

29. This fragmentary section may conceivably be restored to refer to premonitions the disciples experience of the arrest of Jesus in the garden of Gethsemane, and what happens thereafter, when the disciples run for their lives.

30. Or, "building." This apparently refers to the Jewish temple in Jerusalem.

31. Probably thought to be either the name of God or the name of Jesus. Wolf-Peter Funk has suggested that something has been omitted by the scribe, so that the sentence may be thought to have read, "and a name <was invoked/was written on . . .>," or the like.

32. The text inadvertently repeats the phrase "at the altar" (dittography).

33. Or, perhaps, "[the people]."

34. Or, "fast." Here and below, on the suggested wicked actions of some religious folks, perhaps cf. Ezek 16:15–22. The *Pistis Sophia* includes similar accusations, as do other texts with lists of vices.

35. Or, "their deficient actions," "their faulty actions," "their wrong actions"—the Coptic reads *šōōt*, which may also be translated "deficiency" and which functions as a technical term for the deficiency of light in many gnostic texts. If "deficiency" is the preferred translation of *šōōt*, there may be a contrast here between fullness and deficiency.

36. Amen.

37. The translation "this house" (Coptic *peeiēi*) is partially restored by Eduard Iricinschi, Lance Jenott, and Philippa Townsend.

38. On trees and fruit, cf. also *Gospel of Judas* 43; *Revelation of Adam* 76; 85. In the *Revelation of Adam* reference is made to people as "trees that bear fruit," and it is said, "Their fruit does not wither."

39. The restoration "[Your minister (?)]" (Coptic *[pet^e ndiako]nos*) is tentative, and is proposed by Eduard Iricinschi, Lance Jenott, and Philippa Townsend; it was previously suggested in the critical edition published by the National Geographic research team. Note the use of the same term *diakonos* a few lines down on the same page. Also possible is "[The great overseer (or, bishop)]"—so Johanna Brankaer and Hans-Gebhard Bethge—or, less likely, "[The ruler (or, archon) of this world]."

40. Or, "to him."

41. Or, "[those who fornicate]."

42. Or, "fast." Cf. *Gospel of Judas* 38.

43. Or, possibly, "priests."

44. Perhaps read "[wickedness]" (with Eduard Iricinschi, Lance Jenott, and Philippa Townsend).

45. Or, "except the great one, as is its destiny" (Coptic *ettēš*). Perhaps compare, here and below, the description in Sethian literature of the generation of Seth as stable and immovable.

46. Perhaps "cannot" is missing or implied here.

47. The reading is tentative and merits further examination. The translation is based on an understanding of the Coptic as *tme(h)snte ^engenea*, "the second generation." It may be possible to take *tme* as a form of the verb *t^emmo*, "nurture," and read "to nurture two generations" (whatever that might mean), or to read *tmes nte ^engenea*, "the offspring of the generations." The lines on the lower half of page 41 were transcribed by Wolf-

Peter Funk from an earlier photograph and edited on the basis of a new photograph of a released fragmentary portion of the text.

48. Restored by Wolf-Peter Funk and Gesine Schenke Robinson.

49. This teaching about people and the stars assigned to them seems to derive from Plato. Cf. *Timaeus* 41d–42b:

> Thus the creator spoke, and once more into the cup in which he had previously mingled the soul of the universe he poured the remains of the elements and mingled them in much the same manner; they were not, however, pure as before, but diluted to the second and third degree. And having made it, he divided the whole mixture into souls equal in number to the stars, and assigned each soul to a star; and having there placed them as in a chariot, he showed them the nature of the universe, and declared to them the laws of destiny, according to which their first birth would be one and the same for all—no one should suffer a disadvantage at his hands; they were to be sown in the instruments of time severally adapted to them, and to come forth the most religious of animals; and as human nature was of two kinds, the superior race would hereafter be called humanity . . . The person who lived well during his appointed time was to return and dwell in his native star, and there he would have a blessed and congenial existence. (Translated by Benjamin Jowett, slightly revised.)

On Judas's star, cf. *Gospel of Judas* 57.

50. On the pillar of fire, cf., for instance, Exod 13:21–22: "And the LORD went before them (the Israelites in the exodus from Egypt) during the day in a pillar of cloud to lead them along the way, and during the night in a pillar of fire to give them light, so that they might travel during the day and during the night. The pillar of cloud during the day and the pillar of fire during the night did not leave the presence of the people." Also cf. Luke 10:18, on Satan falling like lightning from heaven.

51. Or, "move."

52. On the tentative restoration "[by the (?)]," cf. Eduard Iricinschi, Lance Jenott, and Philippa Townsend, and the edition of Jenott.

53. Literally, "he" or "it." The antecedent of the pronoun is unclear. On Seth as the one who brings water, compare, with Birger Pearson, Philo of Alexandria, *De Posteritate Caini* ("On the Posterity and Exile of Cain") 36: "'Adam,' it says, 'knew Eve his wife, and she conceived and bore a son, and called his name Seth, saying, "God has raised up to me another seed in the place of Abel, whom Cain slew."' 'Seth' means 'watering' (*potismos*). As, then, the seeds and plants in the earth, when watered, grow and sprout

and are prolific in producing fruit, but, if no water is poured on them, wither away, so the soul, as is evident, when it is fostered with a fresh sweet stream of wisdom (*sophia*) shoots up and improves" (translated by F. H. Colson and G. H. Whitaker, Loeb Classical Library, slightly revised, here and below). A similar observation is made in *De Posteritate Caini* 49:

> Well, then, the mind, when it begets a beginning of good disposition and a kind of first pattern of virtue in Seth, which means "watering," is audacious with a fine and holy audacity. For it says, "God raised up to me another seed in the place of Abel, whom Cain slew." The statement that none of God's seeds fall to the ground, but all mount upwards rising from out of earthly surroundings, and leaving them behind, is a noticeable statement that can stand every test. For the seeds that mortals deposit for the production of living beings or plants do not all come to perfection; and we are well content if those that come to nothing do not outnumber those that hold on. But God sows in souls nothing futile, but seeds so successful and perfect in every case that each one immediately yields the full crop of the fruits appropriate to it.

54. Cf. Gen 2:10: "A river flowed from Eden to water the garden, and it divided there and formed four rivers."

55. Or, "generation" (Coptic [*ge*]*nos*). It may also be possible to restore to read "fruit" (with Eduard Iricinschi, Lance Jenott, and Philippa Townsend).

56. Perhaps read "[Rabb]i" (Coptic [*hrabb*]*ei*, an early reading), "[Tell] me" (Coptic [*tamo*]*ei*, with Wolf-Peter Funk), or the like.

57. The *Gospel of Judas* seems to understand the human spirit to be the breath of life that animates people and keeps their bodies alive for a period of time, and the human soul to be the true, inner self that allows the people of Seth to remain alive and be taken up after their bodies die. On the spirit and the soul, cf. also *Gospel of Judas* 53.

58. The word "seed" is added in the translation for the sake of clarification.

59. On this saying, cf. the parable of the sower in Matt 13:1–23; Mark 4:1–20; Luke 8:4–15; *Gospel of Thomas* 9. The *Thomas* version reads as follows: "Jesus said, 'Look, the sower went out, took a handful of seeds, and scattered them. Some fell on the road, and the birds came and pecked them up. Others fell on rock, and they did not take root in the soil and did not produce heads of grain. Others fell on thorns, and they choked the seeds and worms devoured them. And others fell on good soil, and it

brought forth a good crop. It yielded sixty per measure and one hundred twenty per measure.'"

60. Or, "generation" (Coptic *genos*).

61. Sophia. Here wisdom or Sophia may refer to the personified figure of Wisdom or serve as a more general reference to wisdom. There is no evidence of an account of the fall of Sophia in the *Gospel of Judas*. See the discussion in the introduction.

62. The organization and presentation of this sentence follows Eduard Iricinschi, Lance Jenott, and Philippa Townsend.

63. Amen.

64. Or, "daimon," or "demon." I prefer to translate the term as "spirit," since this is the most neutral translation. Cf. the role of the spirit or daimon of Socrates as a guiding spirit in Plato's *Symposium*. In the Greco-Roman world a daimon was usually considered an intermediate being, between the human and divine realms. In Jewish and Christian literature, the word *daimōn* commonly designates an evil demon, a point emphasized by April DeConick and others. In the *Pistis Sophia* and elsewhere, Sophia, like Judas, is likened to a daimon—in two or three languages. Initially Sophia bemoans her fate, saying, "I have become like a peculiar demon (the term of Greek origin, *daimōn*), which dwells in matter, in whom is no light. And I have become like a spirit counterpart (*antimimon ᵉmpn(eum)a*), which is in a material body, in which there is no light-power" (1.39). Later Sophia laments that "they have taken away my light and my power, and my power is shaken within me, and I have not been able to stand upright in their midst, I have become like matter which has fallen; I have been cast on this side and that, like a demon which is in the air" (1.55). The word used for "demon" here is *refšoor*, the Coptic equivalent of the Greek *daimonion*. It should also be noted that Pseudo-Tertullian (an author writing under the name of Tertullian) states in his work *Adversus omnes haereses* ("Against All Heresies") 1.2 that Simon Magus is said to have come into this world on behalf of an erring daimon (Latin, *daemonem*), who is wisdom (*sapientia*). Further, Irenaeus of Lyon maintains that some second-century gnostics (perhaps Valentinians) compared the figures of Judas and Sophia in terms of their experiences in this world (as is to be expected, Irenaeus argues against this interpretation):

> Then, again, as to their assertion that the passion of the twelfth aeon was proved through the conduct of Judas, how is it possible that Judas can be compared with this aeon as being an emblem of her—he who was expelled from the number of the twelve, and never restored to his place? For that aeon, whose type they declare Judas to be, after being

separated from her Enthymesis (thought, reflection), was restored or recalled to her former position; but Judas was deprived of his office, and cast out, while Matthias was ordained in his place, according to what is written, "And his bishopric let another take" (Acts 1:20). They ought therefore to maintain that the twelfth aeon was cast out of the Pleroma, and that another was produced, or sent forth to fill her place; if, that is to say, she is pointed at in Judas. Moreover, they tell us that it was the aeon herself who suffered, but Judas was the betrayer, and not the sufferer. Even they themselves acknowledge that it was the suffering Christ, and not Judas, who came to the endurance of passion. How, then, could Judas, the betrayer of him who had to suffer for our salvation, be the type and image of that aeon who suffered? (2.20).

Hence, in a manner that closely parallels the portrayal of Judas Iscariot in the *Gospel of Judas*, Sophia in the *Pistis Sophia* and other texts is likened to a daimon, perhaps as an intermediary being; she is persecuted at the hands of the archons of the twelve aeons; and though long separated from it, she will return to her dwelling place in "the thirteenth aeon, the place of righteousness." Here, in the *Gospel of Judas*, Judas is described as the thirteenth, perhaps in part because he is excluded from the group of the twelve disciples. On his connection (and the connection of Sophia) to the thirteenth aeon, cf. *Gospel of Judas* 55 and the notes.

65. Or, "[in that place]" (restored by Eduard Iricinschi, Lance Jenott, and Philippa Townsend).

66. This translation follows that of Jacques van der Vliet. Rather than "room," it is also possible to translate this as "roof" (thus, "a single roof," "a thatched roof," even "a <broad> roof"). Eduard Iricinschi, Lance Jenott, and Philippa Townsend prefer to translate this phrase as "a roof of lightning," and they refer to the similar description of the heavenly house in *1 Enoch*. See also the edition of Lance Jenott. In *1 Enoch* the heavenly house is described as large and of indescribable majesty, with a roof of lightning or fire. This reading may be considered less likely, however, on the basis of a careful examination of the ink traces undertaken in Augsburg in June–July 2011 and the lack of attestation of the Coptic word understood to mean "lightning." On the heavenly house or mansion in the Gospel of John, cf. John 14:1–14.

67. About two lines missing. Judas is speaking the following sentence in his account of the vision.

68. Or, "the saints."

69. The holy.

70. On this description of the heavenly house, cf. the portrayal of the heavenly city in Rev 21:23: "The city does not need sun or moon to shine on it, for God's glory gives it light and the lamb is its lamp." In the *Secret Book of John* II, 9, the souls of the holy, or the saints, dwell in the third aeon with the third luminary Daveithai, the place where the offspring of Seth reside.

71. Perhaps compare the star of Judas ruling over the thirteenth aeon, according to *Gospel of Judas* 55.

72. Archons. Or, "Master, surely my seed does not subdue the rulers!"

73. About two lines missing. The clause "so that I may [speak with you]" is partially restored by Eduard Iricinschi, Lance Jenott, and Philippa Townsend. In his edition Jenott suggests additional restoration: "so that I may [speak with you about the holy generation, not so that you will go to it], . . ." (on the basis of *Gospel of Judas* 35).

74. Or, "but that you."

75. Here the thought may be that Judas is set apart from that generation in the sense of being oppressed in this world of mortality. On Judas being set apart from the disciples, cf. *Gospel of Judas* 35. Earlier translations by the National Geographic research team, and Elaine Pagels and Karen King, suggested that this preposition might also possibly mean "for" (compare Crum, *A Coptic Dictionary*, 271b–72a; according to Crum, *porj⸱ e-*, which is the form of the verb used here, may mean either "divided or separated from" or "divided or separated into, for," and may translate Greek verbal forms with these meanings). Now most of us prefer the translation "from."

76. Or, "they <will . . .> to you, that you may not ascend." This remains a difficult passage, and the translation I adopt here assumes, with Wolf-Peter Funk and Peter Nagel, that an ancient translator or scribe inadvertently omitted an unknown number of letters, words, or lines. Such an assumption of an ancient textual error, posited in order to explain a difficult reading that defies easy translation, is a fairly desperate suggestion that should please no one. It does not please me, but I see no other clear option at this time. Originally the passage was read as follows: *senakauō nekktē epšōi,* "they will curse your ascent." The current reading is this: *se<na . . .* (the verb is assumed to be missing)> *nak auō nekbōk epšōi,* "they <will . . .> to you, and you will not ascend." Other readings and translations may also prove to be possible. For example, if the verb *nekbōk* would be taken to be a conjunctive form, as mentioned by Lance Jenott and others, with hesitation, the translation could be quite different: "and you will ascend."

77. Perhaps restore to read "[mysteries]" (with Eduard Iricinschi, Lance Jenott, and Philippa Townsend).

78. Here Gregor Wurst suggests the possible restoration "that the human [generation] (Coptic ge[nea]) will see." An earlier suggestion proposed that the passage be restored to read "that [no] (lao[ue]) person will see" (there are grammatical issues with this restoration). A negative statement is expected here. The following cosmogonic revelation is put on the lips of Jesus in the *Gospel of Judas*, but except for what may be a Christian interpolation on page 52, the revelation seems to be a Hellenistic Jewish composition with a mystical or Sethian perspective. The closest parallels to this cosmogonic revelation are to be found in the *Secret Book of John*, the *Holy Book of the Great Invisible Spirit*, *Eugnostos the Blessed*, and the *Wisdom of Jesus Christ*. For gnostic texts that also are secondarily Christianized, compare the *Secret Book of John*, and the transformation of the Jewish text *Eugnostos the Blessed* into the Christian *Wisdom of Jesus Christ*.

79. The highest expression of the divine is frequently called the great invisible Spirit in Sethian texts. Cf. *Secret Book of John* II, 2–3:

The One is a sovereign that has nothing over it. It is God and Parent, Father of all, the invisible one that is over all, that is incorruptible, that is pure light at which no eye can gaze. The One is the invisible Spirit. We should not think of it as a god or like a god. For it is greater than a god, because it has nothing over it and no lord above it. It does not [exist] within anything inferior [to it, since everything] exists within it, [for it established] itself. It is eternal, since it does not need anything. For it is absolutely complete. It has never lacked anything in order to be completed by it. Rather, it is always absolutely complete in light.

80. Cf. 1 Cor 2:9; *Gospel of Thomas* 17; *Dialogue of the Savior* 140. *Gospel of Thomas* 17 reads, "Jesus said, 'I shall give you what no eye has seen, what no ear has heard, what no hand has touched, what has not arisen in the human heart.'"

81. Compare, perhaps, the place of Barbelo in other Sethian texts (see also *Gospel of Judas* 35 and the note).

82. Or, "it"—that is, the Spirit.

83. Or, "assistant," "helper," here and below.

84. Autogenes, the Self-Generated, here and below. In Sethian texts the child of the great invisible Spirit is often called Autogenes, the Self-Conceived or Self-Generated. Cf. the *Secret Book of John*:

The Father gazed into Barbelo, with the pure light surrounding the invisible Spirit, and his radiance. Barbelo conceived from him, and he produced a spark of light similar to the blessed light but not as great. This was the only child of the mother-father that had come forth, the only offspring, the only child of the Father, the pure light. The invisible virgin Spirit rejoiced over the light that was produced, that came forth from the first power of the Spirit's forethought, who is Barbelo. The Spirit anointed it with his own goodness until it was perfect, with no lack of goodness, since it was anointed with the goodness of the invisible Spirit. The child stood in the presence of the Spirit as the Spirit anointed the child. As soon as the child received this from the Spirit, it glorified the holy Spirit and perfect forethought. Because of her it had come forth. The child asked to be given mind as a companion to work with, and the Spirit consented. When the invisible Spirit consented, mind appeared and stood by the anointed, and glorified the Spirit and Barbelo. All these beings came into existence in silence. Mind wished to create something by means of the word of the invisible Spirit. Its will became a reality and appeared, with mind and the light, glorifying it. Word followed will. For the anointed, the divine Self-Conceived (Autogenes), created everything by the word. . . . The holy Spirit brought the divine self-conceived child of himself and Barbelo to perfection, so that the child might stand before the great invisible Spirit as the divine Self-Conceived, the anointed, who honored the Spirit with loud acclaim. (II, 6–7)

On Barbelo, cf. *Gospel of Judas* 35 and the note.

85. In Sethian texts four luminaries, usually named Harmozel, Oroiael, Daveithai, and Eleleth, come into existence through the Self-Conceived, Autogenes. Cf., for instance, the *Holy Book of the Great Invisible Spirit*:

The great divine self-conceived word and the incorruptible human Adamas offered praise. They requested power and eternal strength for the Self-Conceived, so that four eternal realms may be fully completed and through them there may appear the glory and power of the invisible Father of the holy people of the great light coming into the world. The world resembles the night. Then the incorruptible human Adamas requested that a child come from himself, so that the child may be father of the immovable incorruptible generation, and through this generation silence and speech may appear and through it the dead realm may rise and then fade away. So the power of the great light came from above. She was revelation, and she gave birth to four great luminaries, Harmozel, Oroiael, Daveithe, Eleleth, along with great incorruptible Seth, son of the incorruptible human Adamas. (III, 50–51)

86. Restored by Uwe-Karsten Plisch. The reading suggested by Eduard Iricinschi, Lance Jenott, and Philippa Townsend, "an [aeon]" (Coptic *o[uaiōn]*; see the edition of Jenott), may be considered less likely on the basis of a careful examination of the ink traces undertaken in Augsburg in June-July 2011. On the figure of Adamas, cf. the discussion below.

87. Restored by Peter Nagel and accepted by Gregor Wurst. An earlier reading, by John Turner, suggested "[the emanation] came to be."

88. Or, "for [him] to rule over."

89. Adamas is Adam, the first human in Genesis, understood here in a Sethian and Platonic fashion as the heavenly archetype and exalted image of humanity. As in Genesis, Adamas is the father of Seth and the generation of Seth. Cf. the *Secret Book of John*: "From the foreknowledge of the perfect mind, through the expressed will of the invisible Spirit and the will of the Self-Conceived, came the perfect human, the first revelation, the truth. The virgin Spirit named the human Pigeradamas ("Adam the stranger," "holy Adam," or "old Adam"), and appointed him to the first aeon with the great Self-Conceived, the anointed, by the first luminary, Harmozel. Its powers dwell with it. The invisible one gave him an invincible power of mind. . . . He (Pigeradamas) appointed his son Seth to the second aeon, before the second luminary, Oroiael" (II, 8–9).

90. This is Seth son of Adamas, also in the exalted heavenly realm. On Seth, cf. Gen 4:25–26: "Adam had sex with his wife again, and she gave birth to a son and named him Seth, saying, 'God has granted me another child in place of Abel, since Cain slew him.' Seth also had a son, and he named him Enosh. It was at that time that people began to call upon the name of the LORD." Genesis 5:3 states, "When Adam had lived a hundred thirty years, he became the father of a son in his own likeness, after his own image, and he named him Seth." On the likeness and the image, perhaps compare the lines just above the reference to Seth in the *Gospel of Judas*.

91. The reading "androgynous" (Coptic *ᵉnhoout[shi]me*) is suggested by Eduard Iricinschi, Lance Jenott, and Philippa Townsend. Less likely is "the twelve [luminaries], the twenty-four . . ." (Coptic *ᵉnjout[a]fte . . .*).

92. Cf. *Eugnostos the Blessed* III, 88–89; *Wisdom of Jesus Christ* III, 113; *On the Origin of the World* 105–6. The passage in *Eugnostos* reads as follows: "Some of these (aeons), in dwellings and chariots, were in ineffable glory and could not be sent into any creature, and they produced for themselves hosts of angels, myriads without number, to serve and glorify them, as well as virgin spirits and ineffable lights. They are free of sickness and weakness. There is only will, and it comes to expression at once." *On the Origin of the World* presents a similar picture of angels, "myriads without

number," and virgins, all giving glory: "At the left (of Sabaoth, the repentant son of Yaldabaoth), the virgin of the holy Spirit sits upon a throne and glorifies him. Seven virgins stand before her, with thirty harps and lyres and trumpets in their hands, and they glorify him. All the armies of angels glorify and praise him."

93. Cf. *Eugnostos the Blessed* III, 83–84:

> The twelve powers I have discussed came together with each other, and each disclosed <six> males and <six> females, for a total of seventy-two powers. Each of the seventy-two in turn disclosed five spiritual powers, bringing the number to three hundred sixty powers. They are united in will. In this way immortal humanity came to symbolize our realm. The first one to conceive, the son of immortal humanity, functions as a symbol of time. The [savior] symbolizes [the year]. The twelve powers are symbols of the twelve months. The three hundred sixty powers who derive from the savior stand for the three hundred sixty days of the year. And the angels who came from them and who are without number stand for the hours and minutes.

94. Coptic *phthora*. Compare, with Lance Jenott, Philo of Alexandria, *De Aeternitate Mundi* ("On the Eternity of the World") 9, on the Stoic view of the cosmos: "According to these people it is appropriate to speak of the cosmos from one point of view as eternal and from another as corruptible (*phthora*); thought of as a world reconstructed it is corruptible, thought of as subject to the conflagration it is eternal through the ceaseless rebirths and cycles which render it immortal" (translated by F. H. Colson, Loeb Classical Library, slightly revised).

95. I.e., in the cosmos.

96. Gnosis.

97. Or, "El[eleth]," or even "El[el]." Cf. Eleleth in other Sethian texts; a number of scholars prefer the reading "El[eleth]" here in the *Gospel of Judas* as well. El is an ancient Middle Eastern name for God in a variety of traditions, and Eleleth is considered one of the luminaries in Sethian texts. On the use of shorter forms of names, without honorific or other suffixes, compare Nebro, later in the text, and Addon (in contrast to Ad(d)onaios) within the tractate *James* in Codex Tchacos. On Eleleth, compare the angel who gives revelation to Norea at the conclusion of the text titled the *Nature of the Rulers*: "The angel said, 'I am Eleleth, Understanding, the great angel who stands before the holy Spirit. I have been sent to speak with you and rescue you from the hand of the lawless ones. And I shall teach you about your root'" (93). Eleleth takes on a creative role in the Sethian text *Three Forms of First Thought*:

Then came a word from the great luminary Eleleth, and said, 'I am king. Who is king of chaos and who is king of the underworld?' At that moment his light appeared radiant, endowed with insight. The powers of the powers did not entreat him. And immediately there appeared the great demon who rules over the lowest part of the underworld and chaos. He has neither form nor perfection, but rather he has the form of the splendor of those conceived in darkness. He is called Sakla, Samael, Yaldabaoth, who took power, who snatched it from the innocent one, who overpowered her beforehand. She is the insight of light who came down, from whom Yaldabaoth originally came into being. (39; translated by John Turner)

Note in particular the role of Eleleth in the *Holy Book of the Great Invisible Spirit* III, 56: "Five thousand years later the great luminary Eleleth said, 'Let someone reign over chaos and Hades.'" The passage continues with the appearance of the cloud called Sophia of matter, cited below.

98. Almost two lines missing.

99. "[El (?)]," or "[Eleleth (?)]" (if there is sufficient room for the longer name on the papyrus) or "[Elel (?)]," follows the suggestion of Eduard Iricinschi, Lance Jenott, and Philippa Townsend, connects with the previous reference to El, Elel, or Eleleth, and parallels the role of Eleleth in *Three Forms of First Thought* and the *Holy Book of the Great Invisible Spirit*.

100. On the creator god with eyes flashing, cf. *Secret Book of John* II, 10: "When Sophia saw what her desire had produced, it changed into the figure of a snake with the face of a lion. Its eyes were like flashing bolts of lightning."

101. On Sophia of matter defiled with blood, cf. *Holy Book of the Great Invisible Spirit* III, 56–57: "A cloud [named] Sophia of matter appeared .... [She] surveyed the regions [of chaos], and her face looked like . . . in her appearance . . . blood."

102. On Nebruel, cf. *Holy Book of the Great Invisible Spirit* III, 57: "Sakla the great [angel observed] Nebruel the great demon who is with him. [Together] they brought a spirit of reproduction to the earth, and [they produced] angelic assistants. Sakla [said] to Nebruel the great [demon], 'Let twelve realms come into being in the . . . realm, worlds . . .'" Nebroel is also referred to as a female figure in Manichaean texts. In the *Gospel of Judas* Nebro is referred to without the honorific suffix –el. Here *Nebro* is said to mean "rebel," and Nebro may be related to Nimrod (Greek *Nebrōd*), the legendary character in ancient Middle Eastern traditions (cf. Gen 10:8–12; 1 Chron 1:10). It has been suggested that the name Nimrod may be connected to the Hebrew word for "rebel."

103. Or, "apostate."

104. Here and elsewhere in the text the name Sakla is spelled "Saklas."

105. The names Yaldabaoth and Sakla (or Saklas) are well-known names of the demiurge in Sethian and other texts. Both names derive from Aramaic or Hebrew. Yaldabaoth means "child of chaos" or "child of (S)abaoth," Sakla(s) means "fool." The description of the twelve angels, each with a share in the heavens, probably refers to the twelve signs of the zodiac.

106. Archons.

107. Restored by Peter Nagel.

108. Here, rather than "[S]eth," John Turner and April DeConick read "[Ath]eth," and rather than "Christ" (*kh(risto)s*), Turner and DeConick read "the good one" (*kh(rēsto)s*), as does Lance Jenott in his edition. Jacques van der Vliet hypothesizes that a scribe mistakenly read the word *krios* (Aries, the Ram, as the heavenly constellation), which was originally in the text, as *khristos*. The attempt on the part of some scholars to read *pej(oei)s*, "the lord," rather than *pekh(risto)s*, "Christ," is made difficult by the form of the definite article (*pe-*) typically used with a noun beginning with two consonants. While the name "[S]eth" is partially restored, the restoration is made on the basis of the existing ink traces (reexamined in Augsburg in June–July 2011), the amount of space available, and the connection with "Christ." In the notes within his edition Jenott suggests, among other possibilities, "[Ya]oth, who is called the good one."

109. Here Lance Jenott, in his edition, restores to read "Harmathoth, who is [the eye of fire]," and April DeConick and John Turner suggest the reading "Harmathoth, who is [the evil eye]." In the present translation I opt, tentatively, for Jenott's restoration. On the latter reading, cf. *Secret Book of John* II, 10 ("The second is Harmas, who is the jealous [or, evil, Coptic *kōh*)] eye"). The former reading, "[the eye of fire (Coptic *kōht*)]," is attested in other editions of the *Secret Book of John*. See also the following note.

110. Cf. *Secret Book of John* II, 10–11:

The name of the first is Athoth, whom generations call the [reaper]. The second is Harmas, who is the jealous eye. The third is Kalila-Oumbri. The fourth is Yabel. The fifth is Adonaios, who is called Sabaoth. The sixth is Cain, whom generations of people call the sun. The seventh is Abel. The eighth is Abrisene. The ninth is Yobel. The tenth is Armoupieel. The eleventh is Melcheir-Adonein. The twelfth is Belias, who is over the depth of the underworld. Yaldabaoth stationed seven kings, one for each sphere of heaven, to reign over the seven heavens, and five to reign over the depth of the abyss. He shared his fire with them, but he did not give away any of the power of the light he had taken from his mother. For he is ignorant darkness.

Also cf. *Holy Book of the Great Invisible Spirit* III, 57–58:

He (Sakla) said to the [great angels], "Go, [each] of you reign over your own [world]." And each [of these] twelve [angels] left. [The first] angel is Athoth, whom [the great] generations of people call . . . . The second is Harmas, [the eye of fire]. The third [is Galila]. The fourth is Yobel. [The fifth is] Adonaios, who is [called] Sabaoth. The sixth [is Cain, whom] the [great generations of] people call the sun. The [seventh is Abel], the eighth Akiressina, the [ninth Youbel]. The tenth is Harmoupiael. The eleventh is Achir-Adonin. The twelfth [is Belias]. These are set over Hades [and chaos].

In the list in the *Gospel of Judas*, the second angelic power is Harmathoth; in the *Secret Book of John* and the *Holy Book of the Great Invisible Spirit*, the first two are Athoth and Harmas. The two names seem to have been conflated in the *Gospel of Judas*, as Harmathoth, to allow for the reference to Christ in the previous line. Further, the apparent correlation of Seth and Christ as the first angelic power is unusual in the context of other Sethian texts, although the identification of Seth and Christ certainly is not. In Christian Sethian texts it is usual to see Christ as an incarnation or manifestation of Seth. Thus, in the *Holy Book of the Great Invisible Spirit*, Seth is said to wear Christ or Jesus like a garment: "Through forethought Seth has instituted the holy baptism that surpasses heaven, by means of the incorruptible one, begotten by the word, the living Jesus, with whom great Seth has been clothed. He has nailed down the powers of the thirteen realms. Through this means he has established those who are brought in and go out, and he has equipped them with armor of the knowledge of truth, with incorruptible, invincible power" (III, 63–64). In a somewhat similar manner, in *Three Forms of First Thought*, the divine first thought as word declares, like Seth, "I proclaimed the ineffable [five seals] to them so that [I might] abide in them and they also might abide in me. And I put on Jesus. I bore him from the cursed wood and established him in the dwelling places of his father. And those who guard their places did not recognize me" (50; translated by John Turner).

111. Or, "first of all over chaos."

112. Cf. Gen 1:26: "Then God said, 'Let us make humankind after our image, after our likeness, and let them rule over the fish of the sea, over the birds of the air, over the cattle and all the earth, over every creeping thing

that creeps on the earth.'" This passage is interpreted in gnostic texts and particularly in Sethian texts to explain how human beings both reflect the image of divinity and also resemble the features of the cosmic powers. The *Secret Book of John* describes how the image of divine forethought (or the heavenly Adamas) seen by Yaldabaoth and the archons becomes the basis for the creation of a human being after the image of God and with a likeness to the archons themselves: "Yaldabaoth said to the authorities with him, 'Come, let's create a human being after the image of God and with a likeness to ourselves, so that this human image may give us light.' They created through their respective powers, according to the features that were given. Each of the authorities contributed a psychical feature corresponding to the figure of the image they had seen. They created a being like the perfect first human, and said, 'Let's call it Adam, that its name may give us power of light'" (II, 15). Here in the *Gospel of Judas* (48) compare the comparable place of Adamas as heavenly archetype and image of humanity.

113. *Zoe*, which means "life," is the Greek name for Eve.

114. Or, "advantage."

115. Here and below this phrase reads, literally, "in a number." Could the second instance of this phrase be a case of dittography?

116. Cf. Gen 1:28, on the command for humans to reproduce and rule.

117. Or, "the great generation with no ruler over it," "the great kingless generation"—that is, the seed or offspring of Seth. Cf. the description of the offspring of Seth in the *Revelation of Adam*: "But the generation without a king says, 'God chose him (the revealer) from all the eternal realms. He made knowledge of the undefiled one of truth to come to be [in] him'" (82).

118. God—perhaps the god of this world?—gives the spirit of life to people, through the archangel Michael, as a loan, but the Great One gives spirit and soul to people, through the archangel Gabriel, as a gift. Cf. Gen 2:7, on God breathing the breath of life into the human being, and the Sethian interpretation of the salvific subterfuge leading to the empowerment of Adam in the *Secret Book of John*:

> All the angels and demons worked together until they fashioned the psychical body (of Adam). But for a long time their creation did not stir or move at all. When the Mother wanted to take back the power she had relinquished to the first ruler, she prayed to the most merciful mother-father of all. With a sacred command the mother-father sent five luminaries down upon the place of the angels of the first ruler. They advised him so that they might recover the mother's power. They said to Yaldabaoth, "Breathe some of your spirit into the face of Adam, and the body will arise." He breathed his spirit into Adam. The

spirit is the power of his mother, but he did not realize this, because he lives in ignorance. The Mother's power went out of Yaldabaoth and into the psychical body that had been made to be like the one who is from the beginning. The body moved and became powerful. And it was enlightened. (II, 19)

On the spirit and the soul, see also *Gospel of Judas* 43 and the note.

119. Plural.

120. Gnosis. Here "to be given" may also be read "to be brought."

121. Plural.

122. Here the text reads *alēthōs* rather than *hamēn*.

123. Or, "fornicate."

124. Almost three lines missing.

125. "[Is]rael" or "[Ist]rael" (if there is room for the additional letter on the papyrus)? Compare the name as it appears on magical amulets. Israel appears as a female power in Justin's *Book of Baruch*. Uwe-Karsten Plisch has pointed out that the figure Israel here may recall the patriarch Jacob, who is the father, nicknamed Israel, of the sons who bring about the twelve tribes of Israel.

126. The restoration of "[Egypt]" is suggested by Louis Painchaud. In this context, which calls to mind the story of the exodus from Egypt, compare the reference to the pillar of fire in *Gospel of Judas* 42. The present section seems to provide an abbreviated Sethian interpretation of the history of Israel, from early periods until the time of Jesus.

127. Here the word "and" may be repeated (a case of dittography).

128. The thirteenth aeon as the place over which the star of Judas will rule has stimulated a goodly amount of discussion among scholars and interpreters of the *Gospel of Judas*. The thirteen aeons and the god of the thirteen aeons—the demiurge, the creator of this mortal world below—are referred to in the *Holy Book of the Great Invisible Spirit* (III, 63) and *Zostrianos* (4), and thirteen kingdoms are mentioned in the *Revelation of Adam* (77–82), even though in this text the nature of the thirteenth kingdom is somewhat obscure. None of the parallels cited from these sources, however, make specific use of the phrase "thirteenth aeon." This very term does occur elsewhere: the "thirteenth aeon" shows up more than forty times in the *Pistis Sophia* (and it also is to be found in the *Books of Jeu*), where it is "the place of righteousness" located above the twelve aeons and the heavenly home of the twenty-four luminaries—including Sophia, who calls the thirteenth aeon "my dwelling place." In the literature of antiquity

and late antiquity, the thirteenth aeon can occupy a place just above the twelve (who are often considered to be the signs of the zodiac), on the border of the infinite—a place, it may be, between the world of mortality below and the world of the divine on high, and as such it is a place with a certain ambivalence. Sometimes, as in *Marsanes*, the thirteenth realm may be taken as the locale where the transcendent deity dwells (though the term is used in a different sense in *Marsanes* [2–4], in the context of the thirteenth seal). According to the *Pistis Sophia*'s version of the myth, Sophia, straining to ascend to the light above, is deceived and comes down from the thirteenth aeon, descending through the twelve aeons to "chaos" below. Here in this world she is oppressed, and the powers of the world, including lion-faced Yaldabaoth, seek to rob her of the light within her. For a time, she is prevented from leaving the place of her oppression. In the words of Pistis Sophia, the cohorts of Authades, the arrogant one, "have surrounded me, and have rejoiced over me, and they have oppressed me greatly, without my knowing; and they have run away, they have left me, and they have not been merciful to me. They turned again and tempted me, and they oppressed me with great oppression; they gnashed their teeth at me, wanting to take away my light from me completely." In the midst of her suffering, Pistis Sophia—the wisdom of God weakened and languishing in this world, reflective of the soul of the gnostic trapped here below—cries for salvation, and eventually her cry is heard: "Now at this time, save me, that I may rejoice, because I want (or, love) the thirteenth aeon, the place of righteousness. And I will say at all times, May the light of Jeu, your angel, give more light. And my tongue will sing praises to you in your knowledge, all my time in the thirteenth aeon" (1.50). Much of this reflection upon the thirteenth aeon in the *Pistis Sophia* recalls the *Gospel of Judas* and the place of Judas Iscariot in the *Gospel of Judas*.

129. Previously this line was restored to read "laughing [at us]," but there does not seem to be room for the restoration "[at us]."

130. The wandering stars are usually understood to be the planets. Here the six wandering stars are probably the five known planets (Mercury, Venus, Mars, Jupiter, Saturn) and the moon. The eleven stars and warriors may also call to mind the eleven disciples (apart from Judas).

131. The place and nature of baptism is significant in Sethian gnostic texts, and a clear distinction is made between baptism in the emerging orthodox church and Sethian baptism. On Sethian baptism, cf. the *Holy Book of the Great Invisible Spirit* (also partially cited above): "Through forethought Seth has instituted the holy baptism that surpasses heaven, by means of the incorruptible one, begotten by the word, the living Jesus, with whom great Seth has been clothed. . . . From now on, through the in-

corruptible human Poimael, with regard to those worthy of the invocation and words of renunciation of the five seals in the baptism of running water, they will know those who receive them, as they are instructed, and they will be known by them, and they shall not taste death" (III, 63–66). There follows in the *Holy Book* a long baptismal hymn with mystical features.

132. *Alēthōs.*

133. Almost three lines missing.

134. Literally, "he" or "it." The antecedent of the pronoun is unclear.

135. "Tomorrow" as the day of torment for the one who bears Jesus may refer to Friday, i.e., Good Friday, the day of crucifixion. On the issue of the sequence of events in the *Gospel of Judas*, compare the reference to "eight days, up to three days before he celebrated Passover," at the opening of the text.

136. Or, in the passive, "Tomorrow the one who bears me will be tormented." On the image, here and below, of the one who "bears" Jesus, compare Lance Jenott's observation, in his edition, that this language recalls the traditional philosophical description of the body supporting or carrying the soul. Thus, in *Timaeus* 44e Plato presents the body as that which "bears" (*pheron*) a person's head, which in turn houses the soul.

137. Plural.

138. Amen.

139. *Alēthōs.*

140. The restoration of these lines is somewhat tentative; a verb in a future tense is expected in connection with those who offer sacrifices to Sakla. Other similar readings are possible. See the discussion in the introduction.

141. Probably the other disciples. Precisely how and why Judas will exceed the others remain uncertain. Perhaps it is because Judas is not among those who offer sacrifices to Sakla and die. Perhaps it is because Judas plays a more prominent role in bringing about the apocalyptic events that will change the world forever. Perhaps it is because, as Irenaeus of Lyon says, Judas "alone was acquainted with the truth as no others were, and so accomplished the mystery of the betrayal." A thoroughly negative interpretation, as a few scholars have suggested ("But you will exceed all of them"—in evil), seems unlikely. On Jesus telling Judas, in the context of the New Testament discussion of the betrayal, "What you are going to do, do quickly," cf. John 13:27.

142. The one whom Judas will "sacrifice" is not the spiritual Jesus but rather the mortal body Jesus has been using. This act on the part of Judas, described by Irenaeus as the "mystery of the betrayal," leads to the apocalyptic events described in the following lines. Thus, Irenaeus says of Judas and his act, "By him all things, both earthly and heavenly, were thrown into dissolution." On the true, spiritual Jesus escaping crucifixion, compare the *Second Discourse of Great Seth*, the Nag Hammadi *Revelation of Peter*, Basilides, in Irenaeus of Lyon (1.24.4), and other sources. The *Second Discourse of Great Seth* has Jesus state,

> I was in the mouths of lions. They hatched a plot against me, to coun-
> ter the destruction of their error and foolishness, but I did not give
> in to them as they had planned. I was not hurt at all. Though they
> punished me, I did not die in actuality but only in appearance, that
> I might not be put to shame by them, as if they are part of me. I
> freed myself of shame, and I did not become fainthearted because
> of what they did to me. I would have become bound by fear, but I
> suffered only in their eyes and their thought, that nothing may ever
> be claimed about them. The death they think I suffered they suffered
> in their error and blindness. They nailed their man to their death.
> Their thoughts did not perceive me, since they were deaf and blind.
> By doing these things they pronounce judgment against themselves.
> As for me, they saw me and punished me, but someone else, their
> father, drank the gall and the vinegar; it was not I. They were striking
> me with a scourge, but someone else, Simon, bore the cross on his
> shoulder. Someone else wore the crown of thorns. And I was in high,
> poking fun at all the excesses of the ruler and the fruit of their error
> and conceit. I was laughing at their ignorance. (55–56)

The *Revelation of Peter* has Jesus explain, "The one you see smiling and laughing above the cross is the living Jesus. The one into whose hands and feet they are driving nails is his fleshly part, the substitute for him. They are putting to shame the one who came into being in the likeness of the living Jesus. Look at him and look at me" (81). It is said the gnostic teacher Basilides maintained that Jesus did not suffer, but rather Simon of Cyrene was crucified in the place of Jesus, and Jesus stood by, transformed in appearance and laughing (cf. *Second Discourse of Great Seth*). Compare also the reading from the *Gospel of Barnabas* in the Epilogue, below.

143. Or, "mind."

144. These lines recall passages from the Psalms or, better, 1 Samuel 2 (the song of Hannah—so Tage Petersen). First Samuel 2:1 reads, "My heart rejoices in the LORD, in the LORD my horn is exalted. My mouth derides my foes, for I am glad you saved me." The song of Hannah is employed

elsewhere in early Christian literature, and it served as a model for the Magnificat of Mary in Luke 1. The additional line about the star of Judas coheres well with the astronomical/astrological emphasis of the *Gospel of Judas*.

145. *Alēthōs*.

146. In his edition Lance Jenott restores to read "your last [days have come]. And . . ."

147. Archon. Lacunae remain in this passage; the reading "ministers" (or, "agents," "servants") is partially restored ([*diak*]*onos*) by Gregor Wurst. It may also be possible to read "thrones" ([*thr*]*onos*), an option suggested by Lance Jenott in his edition.

148. Or, "fruit," or "place" (suggested by Eduard Iricinschi, Lance Jenott, and Philippa Townsend).

149. Everything that is earthly and heavenly is destroyed, and the cosmic powers are brought down, as Irenaeus states in his brief synopsis of the *Gospel of Judas*, but those of that generation—of "the image of the great generation of Adam"—will be glorified. In this regard Lance Jenott concludes in his edition (*The Gospel of Judas*, 36), "Far from advocating a docetic Christology that denies the reality of Jesus' incarnation and suffering, our *Judas* assumes what many Christians did, that Jesus had two natures, divine and human, and that the suffering of his human nature alone effected salvation. Our *Judas* interprets Jesus' passion in terms of a soteriology popular among ancient Christians—including New Testament and patristic authors—the soteriology of *Christus Victor*. This interpretation understands Jesus' sacrificial death as a moment of deliverance from oppressive thrones, kings, wicked angels, the world ruler, and the fate of death." While I appreciate Jenott's positive understanding of the death of Jesus in the *Gospel of Judas* as an event that brings about victory over the cosmic powers, I suggest that the *Gospel of Judas*, in good Sethian fashion, stresses the primacy of the spiritual, divine nature of Jesus.

150. Jesus, the new fragments confirm, is about to ascend to a luminous cloud, and the stars of the disciples surround the cloud as witnesses, with the star of Judas in the lead.

151. Here the pronoun refers to Jesus (so also Sasagu Arai, Birger Pearson, Gesine Schenke Robinson, and others). In the *Gospel of Judas* it is Jesus who is transfigured and ascends to the luminous realm. The spiritual person of Jesus thus returns to the light above, and his fleshly body that is left behind in this world below is handed over to the authorities to be crucified. On the transfiguration of Jesus, cf. the accounts in the New

Testament gospels and the *Book of Allogenes* 61–62ff.; on the ascension of Jesus, cf. Acts 1 and a number of gnostic texts.

152. The content of the revelation from the voice coming out of the cloud is uncertain, on account of the fragmentary nature of the text, but the words that are preserved ("great generation," "image") may suggest a positive statement about those who are saved.

153. The reference, though fragmentary, to a "commotion among the Jews" may anticipate the crucifixion of the earthly body of Jesus and the subsequent eschatological events. Compare the passion narrative in the Gospel of Matthew, with its apocalyptic elements, and other early Christian texts.

154. Or, "[they]."

155. Mark 14:14 and Luke 22:11 use the same word for "guest room" (*kataluma*).

156. Here the Coptic verb for "hand over" is *paradidou* (from the Greek *paradidonai*), as in the New Testament gospels. Cf. also the use of this verb in the letters of Paul (see the Epilogue, below).

157. Coptic *peuaggelion* *<sup>e</sup>nioudas*, "The Gospel of Judas" (not "The Gospel according to Judas").

# EPILOGUE

# A Night with Judas Iscariot:
# A Script for Readers' Theater

*In the spring of 2010 I spent another night with Judas Iscariot and the* Gospel of Judas. *By this time scholars had begun to weigh in on the gospel and its possible meaning, and some had turned increasing attention to the person of Judas himself. After all, Judas figures in a central way in the tale of Jesus and his death, so that the stories of Jesus and Judas are inextricably connected in the literature. It did not come as a particular surprise to discover that others beyond the world of scholars also were fascinated with the* Gospel of Judas *and Judas Iscariot. From the moment of the announcement of the publication of the* Gospel of Judas *orchestrated by the National Geographic Society in 2006, there had been a huge amount of interest in Judas and his gospel. Most people seemed eager to find out more about the character of the text and its significance for our knowledge of Judas and Jesus. Some were not pleased with the publication, however, and an international letter-writing campaign was launched, apparently organized through the Internet, to warn the members of the National Geographic research team of the dire consequences for us of our work on the text of the* Gospel of Judas.

*Like Judas in* Jesus Christ Superstar, *we were told to beware of being damned for all time. Apocalyptic passages of woe from the Bible were cited as indications of the punishments to be visited upon the wicked—that is, upon wicked people like us, who brought an ancient text relating to Judas Iscariot to light. Happily, such was not the sentiment of most people who engaged us, and in lectures and Judas events around the world we were greeted by people who wanted to learn more about the* Gospel of Judas. *On that night in 2010 several Chapman University colleagues and I did a readers' theater presentation of traditions surrounding Judas, including the* Gospel of Judas. *Only a sampling of the extensive literature relating to Judas could be used in the presentation; there is considerably more literature in the Jewish Scriptures and elsewhere that informs the development of Judas traditions. That night the auditorium was packed with people who, like us, wondered about this engaging and enigmatic character from the ancient world of Jesus. I wore a prayer shawl and read the lines for Judas, now a middle-aged Jewish man reflecting on his life and legacy.*

This script for "A Night with Judas Iscariot" presents, in dramatic form, issues raised by the *Gospel of Judas* and the other texts relating to the interpretation of Judas. In much of the literature on Judas Iscariot, he is vilified and demonized, but the appearance of the *Gospel of Judas* has reopened the discussion of who Judas actually was as an historical figure or literary creation, and why he has been treated so harshly.

It may be that the time for the redemption of Judas Iscariot is at hand. His redemption could mean a time for some reconsideration, redemption, and healing within the whole Judeo-Christian-Islamic family of religions, which all struggle with Judas, his act, and its implications.

"A Night with Judas Iscariot" was presented at the Wallace All Faiths Chapel on the campus of Chapman University in April 2010. In addition to the readers, the presentation included music from *Jesus Christ Superstar* and Bob Dylan, along with artwork depicting Judas and video clips on the *Gospel of Judas*. The translations of most of the texts cited in the presentation are reedited and adapted from my earlier work, particularly the book *Judas: The Definitive Collection of Gospels and Legends about the Infamous Apostle of Jesus*. The selection from Sedulius is translated by Patrick McBrine, and the selections from the *Golden Legend* and Homer are translated by Jonathan Meyer. Some of the ideas presented here are also discussed by William Klassen in *Judas: Betrayer or Friend of Jesus?*, by Hyam Maccoby in *Judas Iscariot and the Myth of Jewish Evil*, by John Shelby Spong in *Liberating the Gospels: Reading the Bible with Jewish Eyes*, and other authors.

**Singer or reader(s)** Judas's song from *Jesus Christ Superstar*

> Now, if I help you, it matters that you see
> these sordid kinda things are coming hard to me.
> It's taken me some time to work out what to do.
> I weighed the whole thing out before I came to you.
> I have no thought at all about my own reward.
> I really didn't come here of my own accord.
> Just don't say I'm damned for all time.
>
> I came because I had to; I'm the one who saw.
> Jesus can't control it like he did before.
> And furthermore I know that Jesus thinks so too.
> Jesus wouldn't mind that I was here with you.
> I have no thought at all about my own reward.
> I really didn't come here of my own accord.
> Just don't say I'm damned for all time.

**Judas:** *Shalom lakem. Salaam alaykum.* You heard the song from *Jesus Christ Superstar*: "Just don't say I'm damned for all time." You know who's singing that song? That's supposed to be me! Moi! Yehuda, Judah, Judas, Judas Iscariot! The very thought that I would be damned for all time! I'm just an ordinary Jewish guy with an ordinary Jewish name— *Yehuda* in Hebrew, *Judas* in Greek—named after Judah the son of Jacob or Israel. I'm just one of all sorts of men named Judas around here; everybody and his brother is named Judas. My main claim to fame is that I was known as a friend of Rabbi Jesus—Rabbi Yeshua. People know I spent time with the rabbi.

Yet what horrible things have been said and written about me over the centuries! That I turned on Jesus and betrayed him—handed him over to the Roman authorities to be crucified. That I did this with a kiss—though of course I kissed my friend Jesus, as we do in the Middle East—what could be wrong with that? It has been said that I was nothing but a wicked Jew, evil from childhood and ugly as sin. One writer, Dante, put me in the lowest and worst circle of hell, down there with Brutus and Cassius, the assassins of Julius Caesar. Not bad company, but hell is not the place where you want to spend eternity, damned for all time. And this is not funny: my name sounds like a word for *Jew*, and so I became the poster boy for anti-Semitism, anti-Judaism. I have been caricatured with a big nose, greedy eyes, with my hand gripping a moneybag. You know some of the artwork I'm talking about.

My poor mother must be turning over in her grave because of the terrible things they have said and done with her son Judas.

How did we ever get to this point? The first person who wrote about me and my friends didn't really write about me at all. I'm talking about my fellow Jew, Shaul, Paul, who wrote about all of us who were close friends of Jesus, in the middle of the first century, and calls us "the twelve," but he never mentions me by name. He says that Jesus was "handed over" to be crucified, and he uses the same Greek verb, *paradidonai*, that later is translated as "betrayed"—with reference to me, of course. And who, according to Paul, handed Jesus over to be crucified?

**Readers:** Paul, to the Galatians: I have been crucified with Christ. I no longer live, but Christ lives with me. The life I live in the flesh I live by faith in the son of God, who loved me and handed himself over for me.

Paul, to the Romans: What, then, shall we say about this? If God is for us, who can be against us? He—God—who did not spare his own son, but handed him over for us all—won't he also, along with him, graciously give us all things?

**Judas:** I didn't hand Jesus over, according to Paul. Jesus handed himself over. Or God did it.

But about twenty years later the gospel authors start picking on me and blaming me. I guess someone had to take the rap for the death of Jesus—so let's blame Judas "the Jew." And get the Roman Pontius Pilate off the hook. After all, the Greek-speaking gospel authors were sharing their lives with other Romans in a Roman Empire, and they had to get along with their neighbors. So ultimately, they say, the Romans aren't really responsible for getting our savior Jesus killed. The Jews did it. Judas did it.

At least Mark, the first gospel author, keeps his cool. He says I handed Jesus over to be crucified—I betrayed him—but he doesn't say why I did it and exactly what I did. About ten years later Matthew says I betrayed Jesus for money and then felt remorseful afterwards, and so I committed suicide by hanging myself. Luke begins to pile on. He says the devil made me do it, and he goes on to write that I died in a ghastly way, by falling and having my guts burst out. Still later John charges that I am the personification of evil, that I am actually a devil—"the son of perdition."

And it gets even worse, in the next years of the second century. It starts getting personal. Somebody starts making up stuff about me as a kid.

**Readers:** The so-called *Arabic Infancy Gospel*: A woman had a son who was tormented by Satan. This boy was named Judas, and whenever Satan seized him, he would bite anyone who came near him, and if he found no one around him, he would bite his own hands and other limbs.

One day demon-possessed Judas came by and sat at the right of Jesus. He was attacked by Satan in the same way as often happened, and he wanted to bite the Lord Jesus, but he was unable to do so. Nevertheless, he hit Jesus on the right side, and as a result Jesus began to cry. At once Satan departed from that boy Judas and fled like a mad dog.

**Judas:** It gets nastier and nastier. Listen to what one of the church fathers says about me.

**Readers:** Papias, *Expositions of the Sayings of the Lord*: Judas went around in the world as a striking example of impiety. He got so bloated in his flesh that he could not squeeze through an opening a chariot could easily pass through— not even his bulging head. They say that his eyelids grew so swollen that he could not see any light, and a doctor could not observe his eyes, even with an optical instrument, since they were buried so deep in the surrounding tissue. His genitals became more massive and disgusting than anyone else's, and when he relieved himself, to his perverse shame, he discharged the pus and worms streaming all through his body.

They say that after enduring many torments and punishments, he died on his own piece of property, and to the present day that property has become desolate and uninhabited because of the putrid smell. In fact, to this day no one can pass by that place without plugging his nose with his hands. This is how great the flow of fluid was from his flesh onto the ground.

**Judas:** Come on! I'm a pretty good-looking guy. Maybe I could lose a few pounds, but that is ridiculous. And I use a good deodorant.

Another author, who fancies himself to be a poet on the order of Virgil, takes out his thesaurus to find the range of diabolical epithets to lay on me.

**Readers:** Sedulius, *Paschal Hymn*:

O would that Judas had been damned to a sterile womb
and never known his day of birth,
nor drawn the pleasing airs of life with vital breath,
but stayed hidden in eternal sleep; it would have been
        better
that he had never known life rather than waste the one he
        was given;
or better still, that he had lost his gifts of life from the
        start,
being cast to the ground just as dust is blown from the
face of the earth by driving gales and great wind,
scattered into the empty shadows and obscured by cloud.

You bloody, savage, rash, insane, rebellious,
faithless, cruel, deceitful, bribable, unjust,
cruel betrayer, vicious traitor, merciless thief—

are you the standard-bearer for these fearsome swords?
Do you command the sacrilegious ranks that threaten us
with point and spear, as you press your face to his and
    mix your
poison with his honey, and betray the Lord under the
    pretense of affection?
Why do you pretend to be his ally and greet him with
    loving treachery?
Peace never conspires with terrible swords,
nor does the wolf give fearsome kisses to the pious lamb.

**Judas:** As I said, I simply kissed my friend Jesus when we said
hello.

These writers even take on my wife.

**Readers:** The *Gospel of Bartholomew*: We found Judas was steal-
ing from what was deposited in the moneybag every day,
bringing it to his wife, and decreasing the amount given to
the poor serving among them.

So, in keeping with the insatiable greed and the evil
eye of this woman, one day Judas was at home and she
gave him advice in a strong and fearful way: "Look, the
Jews are after your master. Get up and hand him over to
them. They will pay you a great deal of money, and we
shall use it for our life and our house."

The wretch Judas got up after he heard what his wife
had to say. He followed her advice just as Adam listened to
his wife—and he was thrown out of paradise.

Now, Judas's wife cared for the son of Joseph of
Arimathea and served as his wet-nurse. On the very day
when that miserable Judas received the thirty pieces of silver from the Jews and brought the money home, the child
did not wish to nurse. Joseph went into the room and was
distressed over his son. When the little boy, who was seven

months old, saw his father, he cried out, "My father, come here. Take me from the hands of this monster of a woman, for at the ninth hour yesterday they received the price of the betrayal."

**Judas:** Lies, untruths, libelous accounts! It goes on and on—now with a fanciful story of what happened between me and my wife after the betrayal.

**Readers:** The *Gospel of Nicodemus:* Judas went home to make a noose of rope, so that he could hang himself, and he found his wife sitting and roasting a cock over a charcoal fire before eating it.

He said to her, "Get up, wife, and find a rope for me, for I want to hang myself, as I deserve."

His wife said to him, "Why are you saying these sorts of things?"

Judas said to her, "You should know, in truth, that I handed my teacher Jesus over to the evildoers in a wicked way, so that Pilate might put him to death. But he is going to rise again on the third day—and woe to us!"

His wife said to him, "Don't speak or think like that. For it is just as possible for this cock roasting over the charcoal fire to crow as for Jesus to rise again, as you are maintaining."

And at once, as she finished speaking, the cock spread its wings and crowed three times. Then Judas was even more convinced, and immediately he made a noose of rope and hanged himself.

**Judas:** In the *Gospel of Barnabas*, which probably was influenced by Islamic ideas that Jesus—prophet Isa—should not die on the cross, it is maintained that I was the one who was crucified, not Jesus. That's a switch. Here I'm impersonating Jesus.

71

**Readers:** The *Gospel of Barnabas*: In an impulsive way, Judas entered before anyone else into the room out of which Jesus had been taken by God up to heaven. The disciples were asleep. Then the marvelous God acted in a marvelous manner, for Judas was so completely changed in his speech and appearance to resemble Jesus that we the disciples were sure he was Jesus. He aroused us and asked where the master was.

We were amazed, and we replied, "Lord, you are our master. Have you forgotten us?"

He smiled and said, "Now you are being foolish, for you do not recognize me as Judas Iscariot."

While Judas was saying this, a military force came in and seized him, for he resembled Jesus in every respect. When we heard what Judas said and saw all the soldiers, we fled in a frenzy.

The soldiers took Judas, bound him, and mocked him. He spoke the truth and insisted that he was not Jesus, but the soldiers ridiculed him and said, "Your highness, fear not, because we have come to make you king of Israel. We have bound you only because we know that you do not want to receive the kingdom."

The soldiers grew impatient and began to strike Judas with their fists and their feet, and in a rage they took him into Jerusalem. During the interrogation of Judas by the high priest and the council of the Pharisees, Judas said crazy things, and everyone laughed heartily, since they were positive that he really was Jesus and was pretending to be crazy because he feared he was going to die.

Finally, after scourging and whipping Judas so viciously that blood rained from his body, the soldiers led him to Mount Calvary, where they used to hang evildoers. They crucified him there, naked, to shame him even more.

**Judas:** In yet another text, the *Golden Legend*, it is claimed that I killed my father and married my mother before becoming a fickle friend of Jesus and betraying him.

**Readers:** The *Golden Legend*: One night, after a certain Jewish couple named Ruben and Ciborea had performed their marital duty, Ciborea fell asleep and had a dream. What she saw utterly terrified her. With groans and sighs she recounted the dream to her husband: "I dreamed that I gave birth to a diabolical son who became the instrument of ruin for our entire race."

"An abominable thing you say, unfit for words," Ruben replied. "You must be deluded by some bewitching spirit."

She said, "If I feel that I have become pregnant and bear a son, there is no room for doubt: that was no bewitching spirit, but a true revelation."

When, after a time, she gave birth to a son, the child's parents were stricken with fear, and began to reflect hard on what to do with him. They shuddered at the thought of killing their own son, but neither were they inclined to bring up the destroyer of their own race; so they put him in a basket and exposed him to the elements on the sea.

The surging sea drove him to an island called Scarioth. From this island the lad, Judas, was called "Iscariot." Now, the queen of that place, who was without children herself, went to the seashore, found the boy, and raised him with royal magnificence. But when it was revealed that Judas was not the true son of the queen, he burned with shame, and he killed the son of the king.

In time Judas made his way into an orchard to steal its fruit on behalf of Pontius Pilate, but he encountered the owner of the orchard and killed him by striking him on the head with a rock. The owner of the orchard was Ruben,

Judas's father. Completely unaware of this, Judas was given all of Ruben's property by Pilate, and he was united with Ruben's wife, Ciborea, in wedlock. Only later, in conversation with Ciborea, did Judas discover what he had done: he had killed his father and married his mother.

Overcome by remorse, on Ciborea's advice, he approached the Lord Jesus Christ and begged mercy for his transgressions—but he ended up betraying Jesus in his greed for money.

**Judas:** That's not me being written about in the *Golden Legend*. That story has nothing to do with me. That story is about the Greek character Oedipus from the myth of Oedipus.

I'm sorry to say that there are more tall tales about me and my wickedness. But thank God there are also a few other texts from the old days that tell a different story. Like the *Gospel of Judas*, composed in the second century, and found in Egypt fairly recently and now in bookstores everywhere. It's titled the *Gospel of Judas*, but I didn't write it. I don't know who did, but this gospel gives a more gnostic, mystical spin to my story. I'm not saying it all happened like this, but the *Gospel of Judas* credits me as the friend of Jesus who knew him well and learned a great deal from the rabbi about the meaning of life and how to overcome death.

The text of the *Gospel of Judas* opens with statements that make it clear that the story of the gospel centers on Jesus talking with the disciples—and especially with me.

**Readers:** The hidden revelatory discourse that Jesus spoke with Judas Iscariot during a period of eight days, up to three days before he celebrated Passover.

When he appeared on the earth, he performed signs and great wonders for the salvation of humanity. Since some walked in the path of righteousness but others wandered in their transgression, the twelve disciples were called.

He began to speak with them about the mysteries that transcend the world and what is going to happen at the end. Time and again he does not appear as himself to his disciples, but you find him among them as a child.

**Judas:** As the *Gospel of Judas* continues, it is admitted that only I among the disciples had the correct view of who Jesus is.

**Readers:** Jesus said to the disciples, "Let any one of you who is a strong enough person bring forward the perfect human and stand before my face."

They all said, "We are strong."

But their spirits did not dare to stand before him, except for Judas Iscariot. He was able to stand in his presence, yet he could not look him in the eye, but he turned his face away.

Judas said to him, "I know who you are and where you have come from. You have come from the immortal aeon of Barbelo, and I am not worthy to utter the name of the one who has sent you."

**Judas:** Now, I said this is a different kind of gospel, with a mystical, gnostic message. According to this kind of gospel, salvation comes from knowledge, not faith, and knowledge helps us overcome the ignorance that hinders us and enslaves us. So when I confess Jesus like this in the *Gospel of Judas*, I use a term—*Barbelo*—that I know from Hebrew. It refers to the highest God, known from the holy, ineffable name, whose holy name, the Ten Commandments tell us, we should not take in vain.

The *Gospel of Judas* has Rabbi Jesus telling me all his secrets, giving me all his insight.

**Readers:** Jesus recognized that Judas was contemplating even more of the things that are lofty, and he said to him, "Step away from the others and I shall explain to you the mysteries of the kingdom, not so that you will go there, but you will experience a great deal of grief. For someone else will take your place, so that the twelve disciples will again be complete with their god."

**Judas:** Ah, it claims that I will be replaced. In the *Gospel of Judas* my difficulties in this world are described in some detail. You already have heard what people have said about me, and you probably know that I was said to have been replaced in the circle of Jesus's friends by another person. Well, these dark, gloomy times of mine in this world seem to be used in the *Gospel of Judas* to tell people there is a way out of the darkness. Texts like this often teach that something of the light and life of God is trapped in this world of mortality—this is often called the wisdom of God in this world—and we people, when we are in the know, understand that this light and life of God is within us. When we know, we overcome the darkness of our lives, we become enlightened, and we are free in the light.

Jesus goes on to teach me, it is written in the *Gospel of Judas*, all about the universe, from the creation of the light above to its evolution—or devolution—down into this world below.

**Readers:** Jesus said, "Come, that I may teach you about the things that the human generation will see. For there is a great and infinite aeon, or eternal realm, whose dimensions no angelic generation could see. In it is the great invisible Spirit, which no eye of an angel has seen, no thought of the mind has grasped, nor was it called by any name.

"In that place a luminous cloud appeared. And he said, 'Let an angel come into being as my attendant.'

"And a great angel, the Self-Conceived, God of light, came from the cloud. Four other angels came into being for him, from another cloud, and they served as attendants for the angelic Self-Conceived.

"And the Self-Conceived said, 'Let Adamas come into being,' and it happened as he said. And he created the first luminary to rule over him. And he said, 'Let angels come into being to offer worship,' and myriads without number came to be.

"Now, the multitude of those immortals is called 'cosmos,' that is, corruption, by the Father and the seventy-two luminaries with the Self-Conceived and his seventy-two aeons. There the first human appeared, with his incorruptible powers.

"After this it was said, 'Let twelve angels come into being to rule over chaos and the underworld.' And look, out of the cloud appeared an angel, his face blazing with fire and his countenance fouled with blood. His name was Nebro, which means 'rebel.' Others name him Yaldabaoth. And another angel, Sakla, also came out of the cloud. Then Nebro created six angels, with Sakla, to be attendants, and these produced twelve angels in the heavens, each of them receiving a share in the heavens."

**Judas:** This sounds pretty dreadful, this life in a chaotic world with a bunch of cosmic bullies, and we may seem to be without hope of freedom and enlightenment, but that is not so, according to the *Gospel of Judas*.

**Readers:** Jesus said, "God caused knowledge to be given to Adam and those with him, so that the kings of chaos and the underworld would not lord it over them.

"And then the image of the great generation of Adam will be magnified, for prior to heaven, earth, and the angels, that generation from the aeons exists."

**Judas:** And what happens to me? Jesus tells me, near the end of the *Gospel of Judas*, that I will hand over someone or something—but not the real, spiritual person of Jesus. The inner, enlightened Jesus will return to the light above, leaving his mortal body behind. And I don't betray the spiritual Jesus at all.

**Readers:** Jesus tells Judas, "You will exceed all of them. For you will sacrifice the man who bears me. Already your horn has been raised, and your anger has flared up, and your star has passed by, and your heart has grown strong."

**Judas:** The last I see of Jesus in the *Gospel of Judas* is Jesus in his glory, in a light cloud, and my star around the cloud leads the way, beyond the stars of the other friends of Jesus.

**Readers:** Jesus said to Judas, "Look, you have been told everything. Lift up your eyes and behold the cloud and the light within it and the stars surrounding it. And the star that leads the way, that is your star."

So Judas lifted up his eyes and beheld the luminous cloud. And he, Jesus, entered it. Those who were standing on the ground heard a voice coming from the cloud . . .

**Judas:** Exactly what the divine voice had to say you'll probably never know, I'm sorry to say, unless we can find a fragment of papyrus to fill in the gap in the text of the *Gospel of Judas.*

As I said, it didn't all happen just like this, but here in this gospel I am given some credit for being a good, thoughtful friend of Jesus.

Well, how did the dastardly tales of my disloyalty and treachery and eventual demonization get started? Where did they come from? Once they got going, these stories must have taken on a life of their own, fueled by suspicion and hatred toward Jews and by a fascination with the story of betrayal. But where did it start?

My best guess is that the story told of wicked me is another example of stories recounted in the literature of the world about betrayals: about friend turning against friend, brother against brother, sister against sister. Homer tells this kind of story about Melanthius the goatherd, who turned against Odysseus and paid the ultimate price. It sounds like what some people have written about me, and a few scholars think this is the origin of the story of my betrayal.

**Readers:** Homer, *The Odyssey*:

Speaking so, Melanthius, herder of goats, crept into
Odysseus's chamber through the clefts in the hall,
and from there took out twelve shields, twelve spears,
twelve bronze-tipped helms with thick horsehair crests;
and he left with them, and gave them at once to the
suitors. Odysseus's knees and heart trembled when he
saw them donning arms and brandishing long spears
in their hands, so great did the task appear to him.

When Melanthius, herder of goats, crossed the threshold,
a lovely helmet in one hand, and a broad old shield

in the other, caked with mold—it was the hero's, Laertes',
which he bore in his youth, but by that time had been put
away, and the stitches of its straps had unraveled—
they sprang upon him and seized him. Dragging him in
by his hair, they threw him to the ground, on the floor,
    despairing
in soul, and bound together feet and hands with a
    heartrending
bond, hogtying him well—no escape—as ordered by
Laertes' son, long-suffering shining Odysseus;
and they fastened a twisted rope to him and hoisted
him up to a high column, all the way to the rafters.

They led out Melanthius through the gate and the
    courtyard.
They lopped off his nose and ears with pitiless
bronze, sliced off his balls—to throw raw to the dogs—
and chopped off his hands and his feet, fuming with fury.

**Judas:** In Buddhist lore, Gautama Buddha's cousin, named
Devadatta, turned against the Buddha and tried to do him
harm.

**Readers:** A story about the betrayal of the Buddha: Devadatta, a
cousin of the Buddha, became a member of the religious
order of the Buddha, and he attained power and renown.
Nonetheless, his heart grew envious of his cousin, and
he entertained thoughts of replacing him as the spiritual
leader of the order of Buddhist monks. At an assembly of
monks, with the king also present, Devadatta came up to
the Buddha and suggested that, given his age, he might
choose to step aside and allow Devadatta himself to as-

sume the leadership of the movement. The Buddha did not so choose, Devadatta was profoundly upset, and as a result he determined that he would kill the Buddha.

Initially Devadatta got some thugs to try to assassinate the Buddha, but the plot failed. Then he tried to make a rock fall on the Buddha, but the rock broke and a piece of stone gave the Buddha only a minor injury. Then he caused a drunken elephant to attack the Buddha, but the beast bowed down in humility before him. Finally he sowed seeds of dissent among the monks, but the plan to break up the harmony of the assembly came to naught.

Devadatta was deeply distressed, became sick, and at last repented of his evil and treacherous ways. He died while he was being brought to see the Buddha, and in the end he was drawn down into hell.

**Judas:** Within the Jewish cultural sphere—my world—a poet wrote about a close friend who turned against him, and the author of the Gospel of John actually quotes a part of the poem as he creates a story about me.

**Readers:** Psalm 41:

Blessed is one who has regard for the weak;
on the day of trouble the LORD delivers him.
As for me, I said, "O LORD, have mercy on me;
heal me, for I have sinned against you."

All who hate me whisper together against me;
they imagine the worst about me.
They say, "A horrible malady has come upon him;
he will never again arise from where he lies."
Even my close friend, whom I trusted,
who ate of my bread, has lifted up his heel against me.

But you, O LORD, have mercy on me,
and raise me up, that I may pay them back.
By this I know you are pleased with me,
that my foe has not overcome me.
No, you have upheld me in my integrity,
and placed me in your presence forever.

**Judas:** But the story of betrayal closest to me comes from Jewish traditions that are quite familiar. I'll bet that if you asked a person on the street in first-century Jerusalem or some other town in Israel who the worst betrayer of all time might be, that person would say "Judas"—but wouldn't mean me. The Judas—Yehuda, Judah—in mind would most likely be Judas—Judah—the son of Jacob, or Israel, who betrayed his brother Joseph for money.

**Readers:** Genesis chapter 37: Joseph, a young man seventeen years old, was tending the flock with his brothers, and he brought back to their father a negative report about them. Israel loved Joseph more than any other of his sons, because he was the son of his old age, and he made a fancy robe for him. When his brothers observed that their father loved him more than any of them, they hated him, and they had nothing good to say to him. Then Joseph had a dream, and when he told it to his brothers, they hated him even more.

One day Joseph followed his brothers and found them at Dothan. They saw him a long ways away, and before he reached them, they plotted against him in order to kill him.

So, when Joseph came to his brothers, they stripped his robe from him—the fancy robe he was wearing—and they seized him and threw him into a cistern. The cistern was empty, with no water in it.

Judah—Yehuda, Judas—said to his brothers, "What shall we gain if we kill our brother and conceal his blood? Come, let's sell him to the Ishmaelite merchants who are passing in their caravan, and not lay our hands on him. After all, he is our brother, our own flesh and blood."

His brothers agreed. As a result, when the Midianite merchants came by, they hauled Joseph up out of the cistern and sold him for twenty shekels of silver to the Ishmaelites. The Ishmaelites took Joseph to Egypt.

Then the brothers took Joseph's robe, slaughtered a goat, and dipped the robe in the blood. They took the fancy robe back to their father. Jacob recognized it as Joseph's robe. He tore his clothes, put on sackcloth, and mourned for his son many days.

**Judas:** There you have it: in this story there's Judas, betrayal of a brother, pieces of silver, and loss of a son. The story of my supposed treachery may well be the retelling of this story of the most famous—or infamous—betrayer in the Jewish Scriptures: Judas, the Judas or Judah whose name becomes that of a tribe and a territory of Israel. Whose name comes to mean *Jew*. Whose name is my name. It should not be a surprise if a passage or story from the Jewish Scriptures would be used as source material for my story. That is the writing technique that is used throughout the gospels to tell the story of Jesus. And if such is the case for me, Judas Iscariot, we'll have to start thinking fresh thoughts about what we're going to do with my story, and the story of my friend Rabbi Jesus, in the Bible and beyond.

**Singer or reader(s)** Bob Dylan, "With God on Our Side"

> In many a dark hour
> I've been thinkin' about this
> that Jesus Christ
> was betrayed by a kiss
> But I can't think for you
> You'll have to decide
> whether Judas Iscariot
> had God on his side.

**Judas:** The words of Bob Dylan's song strike home even today. Yes, I too, like Dylan in the song, am weary as hell, and confused, and I'm tired, centuries tired, of being damned for what people think I did. But now you know more about me. And you'll have to decide whether I had God on my side.

Peace be with you.

**Judas exits.**

# BIBLIOGRAPHY

Barnstone, Willis, and Marvin Meyer, editors. *Essential Gnostic Scriptures.* Boston: Shambhala, 2010.

———, editors. *The Gnostic Bible.* Rev. ed. Boston: Shambhala, 2009.

Bauer, Walter. *Orthodoxy and Heresy in Earliest Christianity.* Philadelphia: Fortress, 1971.

Bonner, Campbell. *Studies in Magical Amulets, Chiefly Graeco-Egyptian.* Ann Arbor: University of Michigan Press, 1950.

Borges, Jorge Luis. "Three Versions of Judas." In *Labyrinths: Selected Stories & Other Writings*, 95–100. New York: New Directions, 1964.

Brankaer, Johanna, and Hans-Gebhard Bethge. *Codex Tchacos: Texte und Analysen.* Texte und Untersuchungen zur Geschichte der altchristlichen Literatur 161. Berlin: de Gruyter, 2007.

Cherix, Pierre. "Evangile de Judas." 2007. Online: http://www.coptica.ch/ EvJudas-tra.pdf.

Crum, Walter E. *A Coptic Dictionary.* 1939. Reprint, Eugene, OR: Wipf & Stock, 2005.

DeConick, April D. *The Thirteenth Apostle: What the Gospel of Judas Really Says.* London: Continuum, 2007.

———, editor. *The Codex Judas Papers: Proceedings of the International Congress on the Tchacos Codex Held at Rice University, Houston, Texas, March 13–16, 2008.* Nag Hammadi and Manichaean Studies 71. Leiden: Brill, 2009.

Ehrman, Bart D. *The Lost Gospel of Judas Iscariot: A New Look at Betrayer and Betrayed.* New York: Oxford University Press, 2006.

Gagné, André. "A Critical Note on the Meaning of *apophasis* in *Gospel of Judas* 33:1." *Laval théologique et philosophique* 63 (2007) 377–83.

Gathercole, Simon. *The Gospel of Judas: Rewriting Early Christianity.* Oxford: Oxford University Press, 2007.

Gubar, Susan. *Judas: A Biography.* New York: Norton, 2009.

# Bibliography

Halas, Roman B. *Judas Iscariot: A Scriptural and Theological Study of His Person, His Deeds and His Eternal Lot.* Studies in Sacred Theology 96. Washington, DC: Catholic University Press, 1946.

Harvey, W. W. *Irenaeus, Libros quinque adversus haereses.* 1857. Reprint, Ridgewood, NJ: Gregg, 1965.

Hill, George Francis. "The Thirty Pieces of Silver." *Archaeologica* 59 (1905) 235–54. Reprinted in *The Medallic Portraits of Christ: The False Shekels, the Thirty Pieces of Silver,* by George Francis Hill, 91–116. Oxford: Clarendon, 1920.

Iricinschi, Eduard et al. "Gospel of Judas." In *The Complete Gospels: The Scholars Version,* edited by Robert J. Miller, 343–57. 4th ed. Salem, OR: Polebridge, 2010.

Jenott, Lance. *The Gospel of Judas: Text, Translation, and Historical Interpretation of the Betrayer's Gospel.* Studies and Texts in Antiquity and Christianity. Tübingen: Mohr/Siebeck, 2011.

Kasser, Rodolphe, Marvin Meyer, and Gregor Wurst, editors. *The Gospel of Judas: From Codex Tchacos.* Washington, DC: National Geographic Society, 2006 (1st edition), 2008 (2nd edition).

Kasser, Rodolphe et al., editors. *The Gospel of Judas, Together with the Letter of Peter to Philip, James, and a Book of Allogenes, from Codex Tchacos: Critical Edition.* Washington, DC: National Geographic Society, 2007.

Kazantzakis, Nikos. *The Last Temptation of Christ.* Translated by P. A. Bien. New York: Simon & Schuster, 1960.

Kemner, Heinrich. *Judas Iskariot: Zwischen Nachfolge und Verrat.* Stuttgart: Neuhausen, 1988.

King, Karen L. *What Is Gnosticism?* Cambridge, MA: Belknap, 2003.

Klassen, William. *Judas: Betrayer or Friend of Jesus?* Minneapolis: Fortress, 1996.

———. "Judas Iscariot." In *The Anchor Bible Dictionary,* edited by David Noel Freedman, 3:1091–96. 6 vols. New York: Doubleday, 1992.

Klauck, Hans-Josef. *Judas—Ein Jünger des Herrn.* Quaestiones Disputatae 111. Freiburg: Herder, 1987.

Krosney, Herb. *The Lost Gospel: The Quest for the Gospel of Judas Iscariot.* Washington, DC: National Geographic Society, 2006.

Krosney, Herb et al. "Preliminary Report on New Fragments of Codex Tchacos." *Early Christianity* 1 (2010) 282–94.

Maccoby, Hyam. *Judas Iscariot and the Myth of Jewish Evil.* New York: Free Press, 1992.

Mahé, Jean-Pierre, and Paul-Hubert Poirier, editors. *Écrits gnostiques.* Bibliothèque de la Pléiade. Paris: Gallimard, 2007.

Meyer, Marvin W. *The Gnostic Discoveries: The Impact of the Nag Hammadi Library.* San Francisco: HarperSanFrancisco, 2005.

———. *The Gospel of Thomas: The Hidden Sayings of Jesus.* San Francisco: HarperSanFrancisco, 1992.

———. *Judas: The Definitive Collection of Gospels and Legends about the Infamous Apostle of Jesus.* New York: HarperOne, 2007.

———, editor. *The Nag Hammadi Scriptures: The International Edition.* New York: HarperOne, 2007.

———. "When the Sethians Were Young: The *Gospel of Judas* in the Second Century." In *The Codex Judas Papers: Proceedings of the International Congress on the Tchacos Codex Held at Rice University, Houston, Texas, March 13–16, 2008,* edited by April D. DeConick, 57–73. Nag Hammadi and Manichaean Studies 71. Leiden: Brill, 2009.

Nagel, Peter. "Das Evangelium des Judas." *Zeitschrift für die neutestamentliche Wissenschaft* 98 (2007) 213–76.

———."Das Evangelium des Judas—zwei Jahre später." *Zeitschrift für die neutestamentliche Wissenschaft* 100 (2009) 101–38.

Oort, Johannes van. *Het evangelie van Judas: Inleiding, vertaling, toelichting.* Kampen: Uitgeverij Ten Have, 2006.

Paffenroth, Kim. *Judas: Images of the Lost Disciple.* Louisville: Westminster John Knox, 2001.

Pagels, Elaine H. *Beyond Belief: The Secret Gospel of Thomas.* New York: Random House, 2003.

———. *The Gnostic Gospels.* New York: Random House, 1979.

Pagels, Elaine H., and Karen L. King. *Reading Judas: The Gospel of Judas and the Shaping of Christianity.* New York: Viking, 2007.

Pearson, Birger A. *Judas Iscariot and the Gospel of Judas.* Institute for Antiquity and Christianity Occasional Paper 51. Claremont, CA: Institute for Antiquity and Christianity, 2007.

Piñero, Antonio, and Sofía Torallas. *El Evangélio de Judas.* Madrid: Vector Libros, 2006.

Plisch, Uwe-Karsten. "Das Evangelium des Judas." *Zeitschrift für Antikes Christentum* 10 (2006) 5–14. Reprinted in *Was nicht in der Bibel steht: Apokryphe Schriften des frühen Christentums,* by Uwe-Karsten Plisch, 165–77. Brennpunkt Bibel 3. Stuttgart: Deutsche Bibelgesellschaft, 2006.

Robinson, James M. *The Secrets of Judas: The Story of the Misunderstood Disciple and His Lost Gospel.* New York: HarperSanFrancisco, 2006.

Rudolph, Kurt. *Gnosis: The Nature and History of Gnosticism.* Translation edited by R. McL. Wilson. San Francisco: HarperSanFrancisco, 1987.

Schenke, Hans-Martin. "Das sethianische System nach Nag-Hammadi-Handschriften." In *Studia Coptica,* edited by Peter Nagel, 165–72. Berliner byzantinistische Arbeiten 45. Berlin: Akademie, 1974.

Schenke, Hans-Martin et al., editors. *Nag Hammadi Deutsch.* 2 vols. Die Griechischen Christlichen Schriftsteller der ersten Jahrhunderte, Neue Folge, 8, 12. Berlin: de Gruyter, 2001–2003.

Schenke Robinson, Gesine. "The Relationship of the *Gospel of Judas* to the New Testament and to Sethianism, Appended by a New English Translation of the *Gospel of Judas.*" *Journal of Coptic Studies* 10 (2008) 63–98.

Schmidt, Carl, editor. *Pistis Sophia.* Translated by Violet MacDermot. Nag Hammadi Studies 9. Leiden: Brill, 1978.

Schwager, Raymund. *Must There Be Scapegoats? Violence and Redemption in the Bible.* Translated by Maria L. Assad. San Francisco: Harper & Row, 1987.

Schwarz, Günter. *Jesus und Judas: Aramaistische Untersuchungen zur Jesus-Judas Überlieferung der Evangelien und der Apostelgeschichte.* Beiträge zur Wissenschaft vom Alten und Neuen Testament 123. Stuttgart: Kohlhammer, 1988.

Scopello, Madeleine, editor. *Gnosis and Revelation: Ten Studies on Codex Tchacos.* Revista di Storia e Letteratura Religiosa 44. Florence: Olschki, 2009.

———, editor. *The Gospel of Judas in Context: Proceedings of the First International Conference on the Gospel of Judas, Paris, Sorbonne, October 27th–28th 2006.* Nag Hammadi and Manichaean Studies 62. Leiden: Brill, 2008.

Sevrin, Jean-Marie. *Le dossier baptismal séthien: Études sur la sacramentaire gnostique.* Bibliothèque copte de Nag Hammadi, Section "Études" 2. Québec: Les Presses de l'Université Laval, 1986.

Spong, John Shelby. *Liberating the Gospels: Reading the Bible with Jewish Eyes.* San Francisco: HarperSanFrancisco, 1996.

Turner, John D. "The Pseudo-Sethianism of the *Gospel of Judas.*" In *Gnosis and Revelation: Ten Studies on Codex Tchacos,* edited by Madeleine Scopello, 571–604. Rivista di Storia e Letteratura Religiosa 44. Florence: Olschki, 2009.

———. "Sethian Gnosticism: A Literary History." In *Nag Hammadi, Gnosticism, and Early Christianity,* edited by Charles W. Hedrick and Robert Hodgson Jr., 55–86. Reprint, Eugene, OR: Wipf & Stock, 2005.

———. *Sethian Gnosticism and the Platonic Tradition.* Bibliothèque de Nag Hammadi, Section "Études" 6. Sainte-Foy, Québec: Presses de l'Université Laval, 2001.

Vliet, Jacques van der. "Judas and the Stars: Philological Notes on the Newly Published Gospel of Judas (*GosJud,* Codex Gnosticus Maghâgha 3)." *Journal of Juristic Papyrology* 36 (2006) 137–52.

Vogler, Werner. *Judas Iskarioth: Untersuchungen zu Tradition und Redaktion von Texten des Neuen Testaments und außerkanonischer Schriften.* 2nd ed. Theologische Arbeiten 42. Berlin: Evangelischer, 1985.

Wagner, Harald, editor. *Judas Iskariot: Menschliches oder Heilsgeschlichtliches Drama?* Frankfurt: Knecht, 1985.

Williams, Michael A. *The Immovable Race: A Gnostic Designation and the Theme of Stability in Late Antiquity*. Nag Hammadi Studies 29. Leiden: Brill, 1985.

———. *Rethinking "Gnosticism": An Argument for Dismantling a Dubious Category*. Princeton: Princeton University Press, 1996.

Wright, N. T. *Judas and the Gospel of Judas: Have We Missed the Truth about Christianity?* Grand Rapids: Baker, 2006.

# INDEX OF ANCIENT TEXTS

## Index of Ancient Texts

## Index of Ancient Texts